EX LIBRIS

DAVID H. N. DAVIES

MALAYSIA
Death of a Democracy

MALAYSIA
Death of a Democracy

JOHN SLIMMING

JOHN MURRAY

FOR LUCY

Printed in Great Britain for
John Murray, Albemarle Street, London
by The Camelot Press Ltd., London
and Southampton
7195 2045 2

CONTENTS

INTRODUCTION

The race rioting and mob violence which broke out in Malaysia, in May 1969, perhaps marked the end of democracy in that country. In Kuala Lumpur, the capital, for twenty-four hours the whole machinery of government was halted and, for several days afterwards, it functioned only ineffectively. Many hundreds of people were killed; many thousands were maimed or injured. A curfew was declared but not impartially enforced; houses were systematically looted and burned. Refugee centres in different parts of the city hurriedly filled with families who had lost everything they owned.

These riots brought to an end the multi-racial experiment which, for twelve years of independence, had shown signs of being successful.

On the third day of the rioting, in a radio broadcast, a Government minister said: 'Democracy in Malaysia is dead.' Anyone attempting to evaluate the effects of the disturbances both on Malaysia and, in the long-term, on south-east Asia, will probably agree with him. But the causes of the riots provide an object lesson for multi-racial countries in other parts of the world. These recent events in Malaysia are all too relevant to happenings in other countries a long way from Asia. It is not difficult to draw a number of parallels.

The problems which the Malaysian Government has had to face, before and after the May riots, are not problems peculiar to Asia alone. They are to be found in any country where people of different races or different religious beliefs have to live and work together. The riots were the inevitable result of decades of racial friction and the failure of the Malaysians themselves to create a viable communal society. This failure serves as a sad example for multi-racial communities everywhere.

The May riots were, in the main, confined to the capital. The interaction between the different racial groups demonstrates a degree of prejudice, ineptness and failure which will disturb anyone who, like myself, regards Malaysia with great personal affection.

The scars left by this racial conflict are deep and lasting; the vital period immediately following the riots was a time of procrastination and lost opportunity. In retrospect it seems unlikely that Malaysia will ever again be able to return to the kind of communal harmony it has experienced in the past.

The present political issues in Malaysia now need to be discussed, openly and frankly, with full realisation of the fears which prompt the thought and action of the country's racial communities. Regrettably the present government in Malaysia takes the view that discussion does not help. It insists that information about the causes of the disturbances, the casualty figures and the parts played by each of the three racial groups should not be disclosed since this would only lead to further outbreaks of violence.

Because I am convinced that the opposite is true, and because I believe these events have a significance far beyond the borders of Malaysia, I have written this account of the Kuala Lumpur riots and their causes. I believe that strict censorship has exacerbated the situation and nothing is to be gained by asserting that 'a state of calm prevails in the capital'. It does not.

Feelings are still running high in Malaysia. Beneath the thin, surface normality are tensions, anger and hatred which cannot be controlled indefinitely by force and Emergency Regulations.

The account of race rioting must inevitably contain stories of bravery, of cowardice and of atrocity. It is not my intention to include unnecessarily details of atrocities which were perpetrated (by people of all races) during the first days of the riots. Nevertheless, some mention of them must be made in order to appreciate the amount of hatred which exists in Kuala Lumpur today and the irreparable damage which the riots have done to the chances of a multi-racial society.

Nothing whatsoever is to be gained by trying to sweep all the multi-racial problems (which are of considerable magnitude) under some sort of embroidered magic carpet. This account will, I hope, make people not yet involved realise fully the gravity of the situation. Malaysia is the corner-stone of stability in south-east Asia. After British troops withdraw from the Far East (by 1971) and the Americans leave Vietnam, Malaysia's continued stability in the vacuum created by their departure is of the utmost importance. The outlook for the country, if not hopeless, is certainly bleak. Nothing is to be gained by continued silence. It is unwise, so soon after the event, for anyone to think that Malaysia is 'back to normal' and that the riots were of little consequence. They were of great consequence;

they will have a serious effect on the country and on the rest of south-east Asia for many years to come.

Some readers may feel that I have at times been biased and it is perhaps necessary for me to stress that I have tried throughout to be objective. My information has been gained from a wide cross-section of Malaysian society—from people of all races and different occupations. Many of them are friends whom I have known for nearly twenty years and many are those with whom I have worked.

JOHN SLIMMING

Kuala Lumpur/Hong Kong
May–September 1969

ABBREVIATIONS

UMNO* United Malay National Organisation

MCA* Malayan Chinese Association

MIC* Malayan Indian Congress

DAP Democratic Action Party (left-wing predominantly Chinese)

LPM Labour Party of Malaya

Gerakan Ra'ayat Malaysia = Malaysian People's Movement

PMIP Pan Malayan Islamic Party (right-wing, Malay)

PPP People's Progressive Party

MPAJA Malayan People's Anti-Japanese Army

NOC National Operations Council

ICC Information Coordination Centre

CDS Civil Defence Services

* The Alliance Party Coalition

WEST MALAYSIA

| 0 | 20 | 40 | 60 | 80 | 100 Mls. |
| 0 | 32 | 64 | 96 | 128 | 160 Kms. |

THAILAND

PERLIS
●KANGAR

GEORGETOWN
◉ ●Butterworth
PENANG

●ALOR STAR
KEDAH

●Kuala Krai

◉KOTA BHARU

KELANTAN

TRENGGANU

◉ KUALA
TRENGGANU

SOUTH

●Taiping
PERAK
IPOH ◉

Batu ●
Gajah

Cameron
Highlands

●KualaDungun

CHINA

●Kuala Lipis

●Telok
Anson

PAHANG

◉KUANTAN

SEA

SELANGOR
KUALA
LUMPUR
Klang ◉
●Port
Swettenham

STRAITS

NEGRI

◉SEREMBAN

Port
Dickson
SEMBILAN

●Segamat

●Mersing

OF

MALACCA
MALACCA ◉

JOHORE

●Kluang

Muar●

MALACCA

Batu
Pahat

Kota
Tinggi

JOHORE
BAHRU◉

●—●— International
boundary

●— State boundary

◉ State capital

● Town

SINGAPORE

REPUBLIC of
SINGAPORE

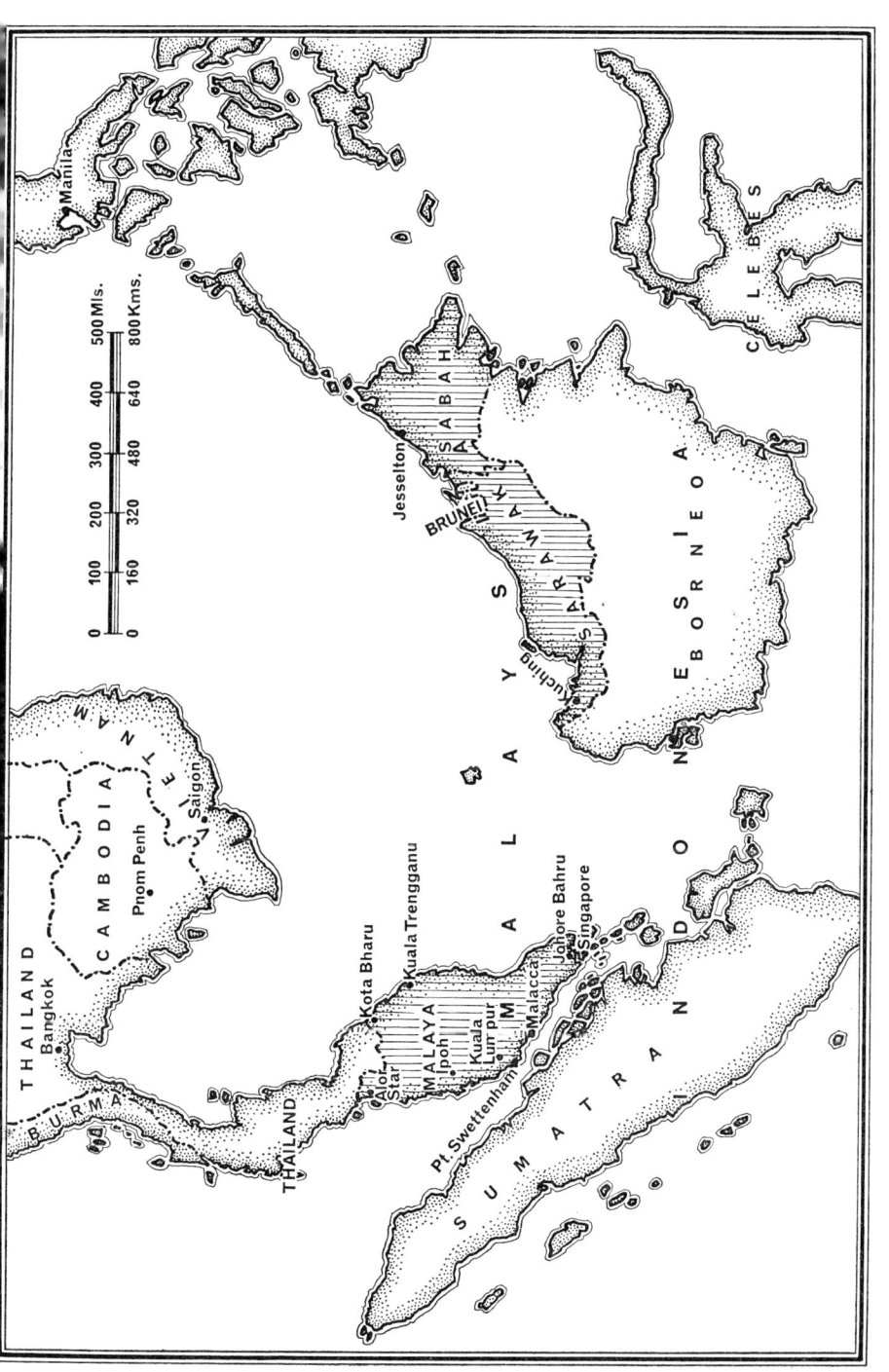

THE BACKGROUND

MALAYSIA AND MALAYSIANS

The peninsula of Malaya is slightly larger than England without Wales. It is the world's biggest producer of both rubber and tin, despite the fact that over three-quarters of the country is dense jungle, sparsely populated. A high range of forest-covered mountains runs down the centre and forms a natural obstruction to easy travel and to economic development between east and west.

Fitting into the tip of the peninsula is the Republic of Singapore, a diamond-shaped island, predominantly Chinese. Malaya alone has a population of more than seven million;* there are almost as many Chinese in Malaya as there are Malays, with Indians forming the third largest racial group.

The west coast of Malaya (where the Chinese outnumber the Malays by nearly two to one) is developed, rich in minerals and served by a good network of roads. The east coast (and more especially the States of Kelantan and Trengganu in the north-east) is predominantly Malay, undeveloped and, to a great extent, an unknown potential.

Malaya is a colourful country. Away from the towns it has a time-less quality and the gentleness of the Malay village people has an immediate appeal to visitors. It is a land of green padi-fields, green hills and valleys, rain-forest and blue mountains. Rubber plantations have been hacked and burned out of the jungle, cleared by hard work and sweat. In parts of the country, open-cast mines and tin dredges have scarred the red earth, leaving it unprotected and plundered.

In towns and cities, people of many different races live together. Markets and bazaars are crowded with Malays and Chinese, Indians, Sikhs, Javanese and Pakistanis. New industries and new factories have made Malaysia prosperous; it is a meeting place for peoples from many parts of Asia.

Malaya became independent in 1957. Six years later, in 1963, Singapore and the Borneo territories of Sabah and Sarawak were joined to Malaya to form the new nation of Malaysia. Anyone

* The population of the whole of Malaysia is over 10 millions (by race, 42 per cent Malays, 37 per cent Chinese, 10 per cent Indians, 8 per cent Dyaks and indigenous Borneans, 3 per cent others).

domiciled in Malaysia, whether or not ethnically Malay, is called a Malaysian (whereas, formerly, on the peninsula he was known as a Malayan). The nomenclature is confusing and has been the cause of much ill-feeling amongst members of all races.

Singapore ceased to be a part of Malaysia in 1965—for reasons which will be mentioned later—and became a separate nation in its own right. Singapore's withdrawal had repercussions in Sarawak and Sabah which have continued to affect the thinking and the decisions of Government leaders in Kuala Lumpur, both before and after the May rioting in 1969.

The reasons for the May riots in Kuala Lumpur are to be found in several decades of communal suspicion and mistrust. Racial friction and conflict are not new to Malaya and have been evidenced for generations, ever since the Chinese and the Indians first came to the peninsula.

Chinese communities had settled in Malacca as early as the sixteenth century but, from the second half of the nineteenth century onwards, the flow of immigrants from South China increased steadily, particularly after the expansion of the tin industry.*

The increase in Indian immigration, which began in the early 1900s, was directly related to the development of Malaya's natural rubber. Indian labour was used on rubber estates because the Malays found estate work uncongenial.

The Malays accepted Islam six hundred years ago; the new immigrants from China were not Muslims and there was no intermarriage between them and the Malays. The Chinese practised a composite religion of Buddhism, Taoism and Confucianism—bringing with them their own Gods, their own languages† and customs, their own style of architecture and dress, their own forms of education for their children. They were not assimilated; initially they made no attempt to become Malayans.

Though a small percentage of Muslims came from India, the majority of the Indian immigrants were Hindus. On outlying rubber estates they lived in their own, separate communities, geographically isolated and, like the Chinese, they were not assimilated by the Malays.

During the first three decades of this century the numbers of

* A table showing the Singapore immigration figures between 1870 and 1912 is contained in Appendix A.
† The main Chinese languages spoken in Malaya are Cantonese, Hakka, Teochiu and Hokkien. These four languages all originate from Kwangtung and Fukien Provinces of South China.

4

immigrants to Singapore could be counted in millions. They came for economic reasons: over-population, unemployment and unsettled conditions in their own countries forced them abroad, to Malaya and Singapore. In China, floods and famine, injustice and maladministration, caused a migration to Europe, America and to Singapore and the South Seas. Not all the immigrants to Singapore settled there or moved up into Malaya. Many of them stayed in Singapore only for a short while before going on to Sumatra and Java but large numbers of them, confident of finding employment, journeyed up-country and settled in the rich, tin-producing areas of the Malaya peninsula.

At the beginning of this century Malaya was a thinly populated country. Apart from the Chinese, unconcernedly mining tin in some areas of the west coast, and groups of aborigines living in deep jungle, the Malays predominated.

Thirty years later it had become a multi-racial country with the Chinese and the Indians together outnumbering the Malays. Some degree of racial conflict and friction was inevitable.

During the war against Japan it was the Chinese, with their Malayan People's Anti-Japanese Army (MPAJA), who provided any kind of resistance to the invaders. They much resented the Malays' collaboration with the Japanese. The Chinese regarded the Japanese as the national enemy; the Malays did not. Towards the end of the war the Japanese flattered and cajoled the Malays, encouraging them to work for Malaya's independence. There was even a tentative Japanese project to create a Greater Indonesia, which was to include Malaya.

During the confusion which immediately followed the Japanese surrender, Chinese guerrilla fighters (who had been armed and air-supplied by the British) came out of the jungle and, with or without trials, summarily executed many Malay collaborators. This reign of terror was short-lived but the guerrillas' weapons remained in communist hands, to be used again during the jungle war which, was called the Emergency.

The Emergency began in 1948 and lasted for twelve years. A Chinese communist minority attempted to take over the country by force. Though they identified themselves with a form of nationalism —during this post-war period when Asian Nationalism was much in vogue—the Malayan Communist Party was, in fact, an extension of the Communist Party in China; it was China, and not Malaya, with which they identified themselves.

5

As a result the racial divisions within Malaya were heavily under-scored, making subsequent racial harmony more difficult to achieve. After some initial hesitation, the great majority of Malayan Chinese committed themselves completely to Malaya but, even though the communists were defeated, it has meant that all Chinese have continued to remain suspect and their loyalty held in question. (The fact that, during those years of jungle war, more Chinese were killed fighting the communists than any other racial group, including British and Commonwealth soldiers, is often overlooked by the Malays.)

For a long time the Malays have feared Chinese domination. They have felt, understandably, that if ever political power passes into the hands of the Chinese then Malays, in their own country, will eventually come to have the same status as Maoris in New Zealand. There are Malays alive today who can remember a time when there were few immigrants; for those of them living in *kampongs* (villages) in rural areas their lot has remained almost unchanged throughout their lifetime. They can see no validity in the argument that Chinese and Indian hard work and endeavour have improved living standards.

In 1950, during the Korean war, the demand for natural rubber caused a boom on the world markets; rubber prices soared. They rose to more than two dollars a pound; the highest figure that year was M$2.38. The attitudes of the three racial groups to this consider-able increase were very different and highlight the differences in racial temperament.

The Chinese rubber tappers went out every day in family strength and they tapped every tree as often as they could; they collected every drop of latex they found and many of them quickly made a small fortune. They banked their money or they bought gold which they hid in their houses.

The Indians behaved in the same way, tapping as much and as frequently as possible but few of them made any attempt to save their earnings. With unexpected wealth they bought new clothes, saris for their wives, expensive brands of cigarettes; they bought refrigerators for houses where there was no electricity and then used them as cupboards; some of them bought second-hand cars to drive to the rubber fields.

In contrast to all this activity and business, the Malay villager calculated that if, when the price of rubber was one dollar a pound, he had to work twenty days in the month to make a living, then,

6

when the price rose to two dollars it was necessary for him to work only ten days for the same money. So, while the Chinese and the Indians tapped more and worked harder, the Malays worked less and passed their time in a more leisurely manner. The Malay has an infinite capacity for enjoying the simple pleasures of his kampong life. The rubber boom was nineteen years ago. Now he is being forced to become more conscious of his country's economy but there is still no indication that he is becoming more industrious.

The Chinese are far more numerous than the Indians and their control of industry and commerce is greater; for this reason the Malays fear the Chinese more. The Chinese have economic power which the Malays resent.

Depending on one's point of view, the Malays could be described as carefree or indolent, contented or unambitious, pleasure-loving or idle. To some extent, all of this would be true. During the last hundred years many travellers to Malaya have been charmed by the rural Malays' way of life; undoubtedly it has a great attraction for the foreigner. In neighbouring Northern Burma there is a saying: 'Tickle the soil and it laughs into harvest.' The same could be said in Malaya. It is a country where food is plentiful; in the eyes of the kampong Malay, hard, physical work, in a tropical climate, is not only a waste of energy but clearly unnecessary.

Again depending on one's point of view, the Chinese could be described as hard-working or aggressive, industrious or ambitious, frugal or money-grabbing and again, to some extent, all of this would be true as well. But the Chinese in Malaya are descended from a people who knew the full meaning of hardship and poverty. They have come from a different, seasonal climate and they want to ensure that they never experience the same kind of misery and deprivation that their grandparents endured in south China. They want to provide for their children, clothe them and educate them and see them well-fed. Family tradition is still strong; they want the family to prosper.

The Malays see the Chinese as a threat to their existence and as outsiders, forcing on them a change which they are not willing to accept. The Chinese see the Malays as a backward people, lacking tradition and history, contented to remain in a backwater while opportunity passes them by.

Much could be written about the Malay and the Chinese positions. It is easy to sympathise with both.

INDEPENDENCE AND THE ALLIANCE

Malaya was granted independence in August, 1957.

With independence, the country became a centralised Federation with a Constitutional Monarchy.* Parliament was composed of two Houses: a House of Representatives (of 104 directly elected members) and a Senate (of 38 members both nominated and indirectly elected). Each state had its own, fully elected State Assembly, its government chosen from the party which had a majority of elected members in the Assembly.†

Since 'Merdeka', or Independence, the ruling Alliance Party has been in power with a large majority. The Alliance is not a single, multi-racial party but a partnership of the United Malay National Organisation (UMNO), the Malayan Chinese Association (MCA) and the Malayan Indian Congress (MIC). The reality of Malay political control, within the Alliance, has seldom been questioned; Malaysia's economic success in recent years has managed to camouflage the political discontent of non-Malay citizens.

Since Independence, Tengku Abdul Rahman's‡ Alliance Government has ruled the country on the basic premise that the Malays should have political power and the Chinese should be satisfied with their commercial monopoly. On this basis an elaborate system of economic advantages has been extended to the Malays. They have been given loans, scholarships and Government jobs (at a ratio of 4 : 1) by official racial discrimination, over the heads of non-Malays.

Unlike their parents, the younger generation of Chinese is not willing to forgo politics in favour of a quiet life and commercial gain. Most of the younger Chinese are more committed to Malaysia than their fathers ever were. They are much more detached from the motherland of communist China than the older generation; they

* Because of the obvious difficulties in choosing a permanent monarch from among the ruling families of nine states it was decided that the rulers themselves would select one of their number to be Paramount Ruler, or *Yang di-Pertuan Agong*, for a five-year period.

† Unlike the American Constitution, which emphasises 'states' rights' and limits the Federal Government's authority, the powers of the Federal Government in Malaya are in practice almost unlimited.

‡ Tengku or Tunku are usual alternative spellings. (Publishers' note.)

8

want to be proud of their citizenship and identify themselves with the country.

The system of checks and balances—which are referred to as the Malays' special rights—have yielded to the Malay aristocracy opportunities of political office and of senior posts in the civil and armed services which the rural kampong Malays do not share. Many young Malays have become dissatisfied with UMNO leadership; many young Chinese are depressed at the prospect that they and their children will continue to remain second-class citizens because of their ancestry.

It has been apparent for some years that racial friction and tensions were increasing. Political leaders, within the Government, were as much aware of the dangers as anyone else but they chose to ignore them.

When I visited Kuala Lumpur in February, 1967—after an absence of only eighteen months—I found even after this short while that people were more outspoken and expressions of racial ill-feeling were more marked.

While talking with a group of kampong Malays, a village elder explained to me that Independence had made no difference at all to his kampong and that, in terms of material gain, they were no better off than they had been under the British. I pointed out that they had a new, tarmac road, passing close to their kampong, which had been built since Independence.

'But who gains from it?' the old man asked me. 'A Chinese contractor built the road—with Chinese and Indian labour—and he got paid for it. Now that it's built, who uses it? The Chinese vegetable farmers—to get their produce to market quicker. The road makes little difference to us here in the kampong. We grow padi. When padi is harvested we take it to town and sell it. There's no hurry to move padi. It can go just as well by bullock cart as it can by truck.'

The Malays listening to him nodded agreement.

'It's the Chinese who benefit all the time,' one young Malay man told me. He was unemployed; he could have found work on a nearby rubber estate but, 'I don't want to do *that* kind of work,' he said.

A Chinese taxi driver, on the way to Petaling Jaya (a satellite town near Kuala Lumpur), told me that the taxi belonged to him, 'but a Malay has to have the taxi licence. I pay a Malay one-third of my takings so that I can operate under a Malay name. A Chinese can't get a licence. He does nothing for the money I give him except let me use his name.'

9

A Chinese waiter in a coffee shop said to me: 'Could I find work in Sarawak if I could get there? You've been there. Is it any better than here?' He was a third generation Malayan Chinese; his grandfather had been born in Malaya. 'There's no future here any more,' he said. 'Not now. Not for my children anyway. We've got to make a home somewhere. Maybe we should all save so that we can go to Canada. We'll never be more than second-class citizens here, whatever the Tengku says.'

This was in 1967.

Ten years earlier, soon after Independence, a land development scheme north of Kuala Lumpur (Perak), made jungle-covered state land available to Malays in ten-acre lots. Designed to assist the Malay villagers, it was an ambitious scheme. Land was offered at a nominal price under a system of deferred payment; once the land was cleared of jungle then free rubber seedlings were given to the Malays by the Government. Only Malays were allowed to take advantage of this offer. Those who did so permitted Chinese to clear the jungle in exchange for the right to plant cash crops on the hill slopes until the young rubber trees matured. After some years, when the seedlings had grown and were in yield, the Chinese could no longer plant cash crops between the rows but they were allowed to work as rubber tappers on these new estates which they themselves had cleared and made.

This kind of occurrence was common throughout the country; Chinese resentment is understandable. Only an extreme optimist could have supposed that Malaysia was not heading for racial violence and that all would be well.

Some observers believed that the racial troubles would break out first in the Borneo States since many people there (especially in Sarawak) much resent Malay domination and feel that they have never attained true independence. Though there is still some residue of goodwill left in Sarawak for the British they feel that they were badly let down by Whitehall. 'We're *still* a colony,' they say. 'We've merely exchanged Whitehall for Kuala Lumpur.'

To those who anticipated the racial disturbances it came as a surprise that they flared first in the capital and not elsewhere, in places further from the centre of government. The reasons why they were confined to Kuala Lumpur will be apparent after studying the results of the general election.

THE ELECTION CAMPAIGN

The immediate causes of the race rioting in Kuala Lumpur were the results of the general election, climaxing a campaign which had been fought, quite blatantly, on emotional, racial issues.

The general election of 1969 was the country's third since Independence. In the first, in 1959, the Alliance gained a two-thirds majority; in the second, in 1964, they were again returned in even greater strength: but the first elections, with the newness and excitement of 'Merdeka' (Independence) and the second, during the insecure period of Indonesian confrontation, provided the government with a unifying factor which held the Alliance together and made Tengku Abdul Rahman's brand of paternalism acceptable. In 1969 no such unifying factor existed. Also, in the last elections, more Chinese than ever before were eligible to vote. One of the requirements for citizenship is ten years' residence in Malaysia. Many Chinese were 'new citizens' who had not voted in the earlier elections.

The Alliance partnership was opposed, in the main, by the left-wing, predominantly Chinese, Democratic Action Party (DAP), the moderate Gerakan Ra'ayat Malaysia (the Malaysian People's Movement) and the right-wing Pan Malayan Islamic Party (PMIP).*

The Alliance slogan, 'Vote Alliance For Racial Harmony', appeared on posters and stickers throughout the country and yet, collectively, politicians of all parties created a situation which called for more racial voting than ever before.

From the outset there was no doubt that the Alliance would retain a working majority. Malaysia had made rapid strides since Independence; it was one of the few countries in south-east Asia that had consistently maintained a favourable balance of trade. The Malaysian dollar was respected in the West. Nevertheless, some government leaders were nervous and apprehensive; they were used to their large majority which enabled them to amend the constitution at will.

* In addition there was the People's Progressive Party (PPP) and other opposition parties which, though significant in some areas, did not command overall numerical support. The communist-infiltrated Labour Party of Malaya (LPM) decided to boycott the elections altogether.

One politician likened their position to that of a wealthy man, accustomed to living on $20,000 a year, who suddenly finds that he has to make do on $15,000.

One of the most disturbing factors, during the campaign, was the insistence of some government leaders that there was no point in voting for the Opposition.

At one election rally, Tan Siew Sin, leader of the MCA and, at the time, Minister of Finance, said: 'The ordinary voter should . . . remember that while a bigger opposition is all right in theory, in practice it means that those voters represented by opposition members will suffer, and suffer hideously, merely to enjoy the luxury of having someone there in Parliament, scolding the Government on their behalf.'*

The Alliance did not seem to set any value on the existence of a strong Opposition. Tan Siew Sin himself seemed to be unsure of an Opposition's function.

The bitterest exchanges were between the Malayan Chinese Association and the Chinese controlled Democratic Action Party. The DAP began to gain popularity at the MCA's expense. Although it campaigned on the issue of 'equal rights' and 'Malaysia for the Malaysians' it was in fact working for the Chinese. The DAP is still anathema to UMNO who regard it as the thin edge of the Singapore wedge. 'The Malaysia-for-Malaysians concept', said the Tengku,† was coined by Mr Lee Kuan Yew‡ when Singapore was part of Malaysia but this led to the separation of Singapore because of the fear of racial trouble. 'The concept is aimed at . . . abolishing Malay rights.'

In the early 1960s Lee Kuan Yew's political appeal had begun to spread to Malaya and in the 1964 elections he announced his intention of ousting the MCA. In this he was not successful but, after Singapore's withdrawal from Malaysia, the residue of his political organisation formed the nucleus of the DAP. UMNO still regarded the DAP as an extension of Singapore's political influence. There is no evidence of any tangible links between the DAP and Singapore (nor of Singapore financing the DAP campaign) but undoubtedly the DAP was in favour of greater co-operation between the two countries.

'The DAP is anti-Malay,' said the Tengku. 'The DAP was formed

* At an election rally in Bungar—reported in the *Far Eastern Economic Review*: May 8, 1969.
† *Straits Times*: April 18, 1969.   ‡ Prime Minister of Singapore.

12

after Singapore broke away from Malaysia. This party owes its allegiance to a foreign power.'*

'For sheer hypocrisy it is difficult to beat the DAP,' said Tan Siew Sin. 'It is obvious,' he maintained, echoing the Tengku, 'that the DAP, which is basically anti-Malay, owes its allegiance to a foreign power.'†

The struggle between the MCA and the DAP for Chinese votes was going to determine how much longer UMNO considered it worth while maintaining a coalition. DAP's success would indicate that there was no point in continuing with the UMNO/MCA partnership.

The Tengku and his deputy, Tun Razak, both warned that the MCA was the only Chinese party with which UMNO would deal. The Tengku's admission that the DAP was the chief threat to the Alliance did much to boost DAP's confidence.

Tan Siew Sin, worried by the prospect of DAP gains, repeated the Tengku's warning. He continued to reiterate the claim that the MCA was the only party capable of looking after Chinese interests. 'The greater the representation we get in the States and in Parliament the better it will be for the Chinese,' he said.‡

The DAP maintained: 'Our party consists of all races, including Malays, therefore it cannot be said that we are anti-Malay. It is the Alliance which is race conscious, since each of its components is made up of one race only.'§

While the Chinese voice in the Alliance was being challenged by the Chinese-controlled DAP, the Malay component, UMNO, was under some pressure from the Malay nationalist Pan Malayan Islamic Party. The PMIP had a greater appeal in rural areas where the Malay villagers found it hard to identify themselves with the 'westernised' city Malays who run the Government. The PMIP, canvassing for additional 'special rights' and Malay one-party rule, maintained that UMNO had abandoned the Malays to rich Chinese and betrayed the 'true religion'. The DAP claimed that the MCA had been unsteadfast and relinquished the Chinese rights to UMNO.

If each partner of the Alliance responded to these assertions it meant that each would have to give considerably more support to its own racial group. This, in turn, would have meant an end to the

---

* *Straits Times*: April 8, 1969. † *Straits Times*: April 10, 1969.
‡ *Straits Times*: 9 April, 1969.
§ *Straits Times*: 17 April, 1969 (DAP candidate at Setapak).

UMNO/MCA partnership; the drift apart, to extreme ends of the racial spectrum, would have begun.

In an election speech, Tun Razak said: 'One race government will destroy the country. This is why the Alliance totally rejects the PMIP concept of an all-Malay government just as we reject the DAP concept of a non-Malay government . . . The opposition parties will only bring chaos to the country.'*

Evidence of political coercion was not infrequent. Speaking at a rally in Kelantan State, Tun Razak announced: 'The Central Government will spend $548 million in Kelantan during the next five years *if it comes to power in the State*. Previously I said we would spend $450 million but I realise, after calculations, that it should be $548 millions.'†

Again, in Penang, Razak said: 'Penang cannot afford to have a non-Alliance State Government. Beautiful Penang will suffer a lot of hardship the moment it opts out of the national stream. . . . This is politics. . . . *We reward support with benevolence*. This is no blackmail. This is straight and sincere talk.'‡

To an outside observer it seemed that the Alliance had no need to employ such heavy-handed tactics. They were sure of winning. In the unlikely event that the Alliance lost its majority, the opposition parties, with no agreed basic political platform, were incapable of combining their strength. Because of the Malays constant fear of Chinese domination the Alliance leaders allowed their judgement to be affected by the Opposition's attack.

'When the Chinese and the Indians joined the Malays in asking for independence they were promised equality,' one Opposition candidate told a rally in Perak. 'Where is that equality now?'

The same candidate (an Indian)§ continued: 'Alliance leaders have said that if we don't like it here we can go back to China or India. We're not going anywhere. We're sticking here in Malaysia the country that we've helped to build with our sweat and blood. . . . The Malaysian Constitution has been changed to give the Malays special rights for ever. Originally it was agreed that Malay Rights and Privileges would exist for only 15 years. But now the clause in the Constitution has been changed to read that Malay

* *Straits Times*: 11 April, 1969.
† *Straits Times*: 11 April, 1969.
‡ *Straits Times*: 17 April, 1969.
§ Dato Seenivasagam: at a PPP rally in Ipoh. *Straits Times*: 11 April, 1969.

14

rights shall remain as long as the Yang di-Pertuan Agong desires. If I know it, that will be for ever.'

Malay 'special rights'—as defined in Section 153 of the Constitution—have done little to improve the kampong Malays' economic position. The significance of 'special rights' is mainly symbolic, assuring the Malays that it is their country and that, though the Chinese control industry and commerce, they still have political power, Islam and their national language left to them. Any Chinese threat, real or imagined, to these 'special rights' is a threat to Malay survival and they react quickly, in desperation.

At another rally the DAP candidate demanded of his opponent: 'Does my opponent support the Alliance policy of dividing Malaysians into Malays and non-Malays and will he have the courage to denounce publicly this policy which has made his children second-class citizens?'*

One month before Polling Day, Tan Siew Sin—with more political acumen than he has displayed subsequently—said: 'Any increase for Chinese support will aggravate Malay fears. . . . The danger of this election is that the Chinese will vote for the DAP while the Malays will vote for the PMIP. This is an inflamable situation since it could mean the polarisation of Malaysian politics into two extremes—Malay racialism and Chinese chauvinism. . . . Any marginal success the DAP might achieve in the coming elections will only bring about Sino-Malay tension. . . Any increase of Chinese support for the DAP would aggravate Malay fears and suspicions because the DAP is openly and unashamedly anti-Malay'.†

For several months the campaign was fought on racial issues and tensions increased. During the last weeks the Labour Party of Malaya (LPM) called on all voters to boycott the election. The extreme left-wing Labour Party is communist-infiltrated. At one time it was the major component of the Socialist Front (which, in 1964, captured 14 per cent of the votes). In April and early May nobody knew what the effect of the boycott would be on the electorate; some observers believed it could influence as many as 20 per cent of the voters.

As the results showed, it made little difference; the Labour Party's boycott call was ignored by most of the Chinese.

* *Straits Times*: 9 April.
† Speaking to the Harbour Labourers' Union, Malacca: *Straits Times*, 17 April 1969.

THE GENERAL ELECTIONS

Before examining the results of the general elections it is necessary to record an incident of some significance which occurred on the eve of Polling Day.

A young Chinese member of the Labour Party was found painting 'Boycott the Elections' on a wall in Kepong (near Kuala Lumpur). He was shot and killed by a police detective. The police assertion that the youth had been killed in self-defence was derided since he was shot through the head from behind. Surprised by a police patrol, he probably started to run away and did not stop when they challenged him. Many people in no way connected with the Labour Party and with no left-wing leanings regarded this as unnecessarily brutal police action.

On Friday, May 9—the day before Polling Day—the police gave permission for the body to be carried in a funeral procession through the streets of Kuala Lumpur. An estimated 3,000 supporters paraded behind the body (which was not enclosed in a coffin) for several hours and, ignoring the official 'permitted' route, snaked their way at will through other parts of town, shouting the thoughts of Mao and waving communist banners and posters. Most of these slogans were written in Chinese; some were in Tamil script. None was in Malay.

At cross-roads and T-junctions the procession was halted by its own organisers, while various soap-box orators addressed the crowd. Mao-Thought in Malaya appeals only to the most fanatical; the orators were hard-core communists. Traffic came to a standstill; many Malay, Chinese and Indian shops along the route put up their shutters; shoppers hurried home and there was much confusion in some places. In the humid, midday heat, with tempers frayed, it is surprising that the confusion was not worse; but, in retrospect, for these reasons, bystanders think that they remember a much larger procession, of far greater numbers.

Some—who agree that they did not actually see the procession themselves but hurried away 'for fear of trouble'—say that it was at least five miles long and more than 10,000 took part. This is gross exaggeration but it indicates the extent of the rumours which still circulate about the communist demonstration. The police estimate that the procession was 'about 400 yards long to begin with. It increased in size as it went along but there were never more than 3,000 people, mostly Chinese, by the time it was all over.'

Foreign correspondents described it as one of the quietest communist demonstrations on record.

The police allowed this funeral procession to move wherever it wanted. They made no attempt to stop it and generally behaved with admirable restraint. Riot squads were kept out of sight, in side streets; there were no violent incidents and what could have become an ugly situation was handled intelligently.

Any connection between this communist parade and the savage race rioting which broke out four days afterwards is, at best, tenuous. The communists were certainly not responsible for the mob-violence and slaughter which came later; there is no evidence that the communists had any success in exploiting the situation once the disturbances had begun, despite the initial contention of Alliance ministers that the riots were inspired by 'communist-terrorist elements'.

*   *   *   *   *

The general elections in West Malaysia were held on Saturday, May 10. For many, the results came as a surprise and a shock.

The Democratic Action Party (DAP) and the Gerakan Ra'ayat Malaysia succeeded in capturing much support, at the expense of the Malayan Chinese Association. The MCA received a massive vote of No Confidence from the Chinese community; they retained only 13 of their 27 seats. Out of 33 MCA parliamentary candidates, 20 were defeated.

The right-wing Pan Malayan Islamic Party (PMIP) also made marked gains at the expense of the United Malay National Organisation (UMNO), especially in the north and north-west.

When the results were announced on May 11 it was apparent that the Alliance Government (which had held 89 West Malaysian seats in the old Parliament) had won only 66 seats and that the Opposition had increased its strength from 14, in the old House, to at least 37 in the new. All the Alliance ministers who retained their seats were returned with a much reduced majority. (The Tengku's majority in his constituency in Kedah State was cut from 11,000 to

3,000 although this is a predominantly Malay area.) One Malay and two Chinese ministers lost their seats.

At the end of the count, on May 11, the results were:

	Parliament	State
Alliance	76*	167
PMIP	12	40
DAP	13	31
Gerakan	8	26
PPP	4	12

31 Parliament seats were still to be decided (24 in Sarawak, 6 in Sabah and 1 in Malacca).

The Malay PMIP was the only Opposition party which was exclusive to one racial group. The 25 seats won by the other three Opposition parties went to 15 Chinese, 8 Indians and 2 Malays. Even the DAP had four non-Chinese among its 13 successful candidates.

At State level the Alliance lost Penang to Gerakan and Perak to the PPP (which was in a position to form a coalition with other Opposition parties). Of greater significance, it reached a deadlock in the State of Selangor, where the combined Opposition strength equalled its own.

Despite these setbacks the Government had a clear working majority and was assured of another five years in office. As one observer has been much quoted as saying: 'The Alliance politicians won the election but lost their heads.'

Malaysia was closer than it had ever been to having an effective, democratic government during the two days which followed the election. An articulate Opposition had emerged through a totally democratic process but the results shocked the Malays who felt that the whole political system had been severely jolted and that their own position was in danger. The Malays' fear of Chinese domination increased sharply as the election results were announced.

Opposition supporters were equally surprised at their successes, which were beyond their expectation. The Chinese population of Malaysia is almost 40% of the whole; for the first time since Independence it appeared to them that they were going to have a significant voice in national politics. They had shown their dissatisfaction with the MCA which, they felt, had never adequately

* 66 which were won on election day plus 10, from Sabah, won on Nomination Day.

18

represented Chinese interests; now, at last, they believed they could make themselves heard. Overjoyed at their success, they staged exuberant, noisy victory parades in celebration.

These parades and demonstrations must be regarded as a contributing factor when considering the immediate causes of the rioting and bloodshed which were to follow but it would be wrong to suppose that they were the main cause of the disturbances. Even if they were, this can in no way excuse the savagery of the Malays' reaction. Gerakan's parade, with posters and slogans, was held, with police permission, on Monday evening (May 12). Malay feeling, already much roused, was inflamed still further as a result but there is considerable evidence to show that dissidents from Selangor's UMNO party were planning a demonstration of their own (with the intention of 'teaching the Chinese a lesson')* more than twenty-four hours before the Gerakan victory parade took place.

The Tengku described the results as 'a major setback for the Alliance'. In his first major speech after the election he said: 'Malaysia is a new country and it therefore follows that the course we are taking is not an easy one. We foresee difficult times ahead of us. Like all new countries we have to overcome ignorance, with all its prejudices, fears and suspicions.'†

Tan Siew Sin, speaking to the press after the results were announced, said: 'It is essential that communal feelings generated during the campaign should be damped down because this is the one thing the nation cannot afford. The success of parties which played on communalism during the campaign may be significant but we hope that these tactics will be discontinued now that the election is over.'‡

These were commendable sentiments but Tan Siew Sin was forgetting that while he accused the Opposition of using communal appeal, he himself had done very much the same thing when he called on all Chinese voters not to split the Chinese vote.

*   *   *   *   *

The severe drubbing that the Malayan Chinese Association received from the electorate meant, inevitably, that the MCA became discredited within the Alliance.

* A police officer's comment.
† at Alor Star, Kedah (*Straits Times*: 13 May, 1969).
‡ In Malacca (*Straits Times*: 12 May).

The Malay 'ultras' (i.e. the extremists in UMNO who have always been in favour of a Malay, one-party Government) immediately blamed the election defeats on Tan Siew Sin, the MCA's President. Ignoring the fact that many UMNO candidates had been badly trounced in the elections, UMNO extremists believed that their case had been strengthened by the MCA's poor showing. Seriously alarmed by Opposition Chinese successes, they were now, more than ever, in favour of an UMNO 'go-it-alone' Government.

On Tuesday morning (May 13) the MCA Central Working Committee held an emergency meeting, presided over by Tan Siew Sin. Before the meeting began Tan almost certainly knew the views of the UMNO 'ultras'; with equal certainty he also knew that, in the new cabinet, he would no longer be Minister of Finance and that he was to be replaced by a Malay. (This had been common gossip in Kuala Lumpur for several weeks beforehand.) It seems unlikely that the Malayan Chinese Association was actually forced out of the Alliance, as some people now suggest, but they were certainly reprimanded for their poor showing and made to feel unwelcome.

Tan Siew Sin is known to be an unpredictable man of moods. To what extent he was responsible for the decision to withdraw from the Government is a matter for conjecture but it was decided at the meeting that, 'since the Chinese in the country have rejected the MCA', it would withdraw from the Government but continue to remain within the Alliance. It would decline to accept 'any appointment in the Cabinet or in the Federal Government or in the executive councils of the State Assemblies'.*

A press release was issued by the MCA to this effect, at 2 p.m. It was broadcast by Radio Malaysia in the evening but by that time the rioting had already started. It was front page headlines in the *Straits Times* the following morning (May 14) but, because of the curfew, this edition was poorly distributed.

Commenting on the MCA decision to withdraw, Tun Razak (the deputy Prime Minister) said, on Tuesday afternoon: 'This means that there will be no Chinese representation within the Government but the Government itself will go on. We told the electorate that if they did not vote MCA there will be no Chinese representatives in the Government. Now there will be none at all.'†

Tun Razak's comments implied a certain satisfaction; his attitude reflected the views of other Malay leaders who, as yet, were not

* *Straits Times*: May 14, 1969.   † *Straits Times*: May 14, 1969.

20

capable of anticipating the consequences of the MCA decision. The MCA pull-out served to encourage the UMNO extremists. Razak is a 'moderate' within UMNO; he should have seen the danger signs more quickly and reacted to them. As it was, he did nothing. Neither did any other UMNO minister.

It is not easy to assess the initial impact of the MCA withdrawal on the Chinese community. In retrospect it was a tragic decision, probably made in a fit of pique, but it cannot have had much effect on the first night's rioting since there was not enough time for the general public to hear of it. On the second and third days of the disturbances it can only have served to damage further the morale of the Chinese, already near its nadir, since the Chinese community felt that any Chinese in the Government, even the MCA, would be better than no representation at all.

THE RIOTS IN
KUALA LUMPUR

THE RIOTS

The rioting began on Tuesday evening, May 13, when a group of Malays came out from a house in Princes Road and, quite literally, ran amok. A lorry was stopped and set alight. A taxi was overturned and burned; the Chinese driver, as he tried to scramble clear, was cut down with a parang and thrown back into the burning vehicle.

In Kuala Lumpur today there is so much hatred, accusation and wild rumour that it is difficult to sift through it all in an endeavour to apportion blame for the disturbances with any degree of certainty. However, Dato Harun bin Haji Idris, the Mentri Besar (Chief Minister) of Selangor, together with other local UMNO officials, must be held responsible for encouraging and organising the UMNO demonstration which started the race riots. Today the Malays speak of him with pride; the Chinese with bitterness.

During the election campaign, Dato Harun was roughly received by the crowds at some of the Alliance rallies. On at least one occasion he was prevented from speaking and booed off the platform. He is not popular among the non-Malays in the Kuala Lumpur area nor in the rest of Selangor. On Sunday morning (May 11) when the election results were known, it was clear that Harun's political future was in some doubt. The Alliance had won only 14 of Selangor's 28 seats but Dato Harun, as Mentri Besar, affirmed his intention of forming a State Government.

The Opposition parties demanded another poll, to be held within a week, hoping for a decisive victory which would oust Dato Harun and end the deadlock. If the Opposition had been successful in Selangor, then, for the first time, the Mentri Besar would not have been a Malay. However, according to the State constitution: 'No person shall be appointed Mentri Besar unless he is of the Malay race and professes Islam as his religion.'

Always frightened by the spectre of Chinese domination, the Malays decided that they had to 'put the Chinese in their place'.* The planning for an UMNO demonstration, 'to teach the Chinese

---

* According to a senior police officer's assessment.

25

a lesson,' began on Sunday afternoon when the election results were known to everyone.

The Mentri Besar's house is in Princes Road, bordering a Malay area on the northern edge of Kuala Lumpur, called Kampong Bahru. The first lorryload of young Malays reached Kampong Bahru early on Sunday evening. On Monday (May 12) further groups of Malays arrived in Kampong Bahru, by lorry, from outlying areas of Selangor State.

On Sunday night, during a spontaneous demonstration and on Monday evening, during the Opposition parties' victory parade, uncontrolled groups of Chinese* gathered outside Harun's house shouting insults and obscenities. These were young hooligans, many of them in their teens and not of voting age, and their behaviour created much ill-will. They shouted and chanted: 'Harun out! Malays out! The Malays are finished! The Chinese are going to run the country!'

Those who maintain that this riff-raff crowd was directly responsible for aggravating the situation and causing the riots which followed the next day are overlooking the fact that groups of young Malays, from rural areas, were already gathering in Kampong Bahru. Tuesday's political demonstration by UMNO was already being planned before the Opposition victory parades took place, and both urban and rural Malays were preparing for it.

Too many people tell stories of the Kampong Bahru preparations for them to be dismissed as mere rumour. Residents who have lived in this area of Kuala Lumpur for many years report seeing the streets full of 'Malays from out of town' carrying knives, parangs and spears. One diplomat described these as 'villains' weapons'.

That morning (May 13), while Tengku Abdul Rahman was flying back to the capital from Kedah, ready to announce the composition of his 'more dynamic and progressive Cabinet', and while the Malayan Chinese Association was holding its emergency meeting, Malays from out of town continued to reach Kampong Bahru and started to gather in the compound of the Mentri Besar's house.

The same morning, Dato Harun asked for police permission to hold UMNO's political procession that night. This was refused by the police.

When this happened, Dato Harun announced that the procession would take place as planned and that he himself, as Mentri Besar, would sign the police permit. During the morning and the afternoon

* These crowds were mostly Chinese but did include numbers of young Indians.

(May 13) young Malays continued to arrive at Harun's compound from Morib (Harun's own constituency), Banting and other parts of Selangor State.

I talked with one Malay (a Kuala Lumpur resident) who was adamant that Malays from his own kampong, near Telok Anson (Perak), were present in Harun's house by Tuesday afternoon. This is just possible, but I found no evidence to support the contention that rural Malays were arriving from as far away as Kelantan, Perlis and Johore.

At least three Chinese, living close to Harun's house, claim that they were warned by Malay servants, as early as 11.30 a.m., that they should leave the neighbourhood 'because there is going to be trouble tonight'.

A Chinese family would usually employ Chinese servants in the home but the syce (driver) and the gardener could be Malay. One Chinese family, who have employed the same driver for more than twenty years, found that 'he had to return to his kampong early that morning because his grandmother was sick'. He left at a moment's notice, without mentioning any impending trouble, and did not return until three weeks later.

At midday a *kenduri* (feast) was held in Dato Harun's house which one Chinese business man attended by accident. He appears to have been a man of swift action but little courage. Alarmed by the Malays' preparations and aggressiveness he left before the kenduri was over. He bundled his wife and family into a car, locked his house and drove out of town without pausing to mention his fears to his Chinese friends. His house was burned down by Malays that night.

Between 3 and 5 p.m. many people in the vicinity knew that there was going to be trouble; some Chinese received warning telephone calls from 'friends in the police'. Some heeded the warnings and went home early; others did not and regretted it.

Two senior police officers went to see Dato Harun in his house during the afternoon and again suggested to him that it would be unwise to go ahead with the political demonstration. Referring to the Malays in the compound they told him that 'these people outside are bent on mischief', but Dato Harun still insisted that it would be a peaceful demonstration, no more than a show of force, and he could control it.

Shortly before 6.30 p.m. (Tuesday May 13) this 'peaceful' demonstration left Dato Harun's house in Princes Road and began to attack Chinese passers-by. Not all the Malays were armed, as they left the compound; some acquired weapons later. Dato Harun must have known that many of the Malays were carrying parangs, spears and sticks; he could have prevented the demonstration from taking place, had he so wished, instead of encouraging it. He insisted that it would be a peaceful demonstration and that he could control it when, lamentably, it was not and he could not.

Much later that evening, sometime before 9 o'clock, Dato Harun himself telephoned a newspaper office in Kuala Lumpur and asked the editor to use his influence in bringing his 'situation' to the notice of the police. By this time his own house was in some danger from a Chinese mob (if not in fact, at least an attack was rumoured) and he was unable himself to contact the police by telephone.

This would suggest that, since he disregarded police advice, the police were prepared to let him chafe for the time being, but no police officer now will allow anyone to infer that this is what happened.

The ferocity and savageness of the Malays in the first clashes seems to have surprised everyone. There is no indication whatsoever that any Alliance ministers were in the least aware of what was likely to happen. The rioting took them completely by surprise.

The question which remains unanswered is: why was the Government taken by surprise when so many people, police and civilians alike, were fully aware of what was going to happen, several hours before the slaughter began?

Dato Harun's involvement with the planned demonstration is beyond question; other UMNO officials must share the complicity and the responsibility with him. At no time since the disturbance has any member of the Government commented publicly on the part played by Dato Harun, the Mentri Basar, or said in public that it was the Malays and not the Chinese who were at fault.

At a press conference on May 17, Tun Razak was asked by members of the foreign press how the rioting in Kuala Lumpur had started. In reply, he said: 'The disturbances broke out outside the residence of the Mentri Besar. I will not say what group of people was involved. They were Malaysian citizens and Malaysians were killed.'

MAY 13–MAY 30

The disturbances in Kuala Lumpur can be divided into three phases:

Phase I: The first 24 hours, from the outbreak of the rioting on Tuesday evening (May 13) until the Proclamation of a state of emergency on Wednesday (May 14). During this first phase the machinery of Government broke down.

Phase II: The next three days, up until the formation of the National Operations Council under Tun Razak (which was announced on Saturday night, May 17). During this second phase the Government attempted to regain control of a situation which was completely out of hand.

Phase III: From the formation of the National Operations Council onwards. During this third phase the Government had regained control and began the task of bringing the city back to apparent normality.

PHASE I: TUESDAY MAY 13–MAY 14

The UMNO demonstration disintegrated into a rioting mob shortly before 6.30 p.m. Soon afterwards, Malays armed with parangs and spears left Kampong Bahru and entered the north end of Batu Road. Cars and buses were burned; Chinese shops were set on fire.

Initially, many Chinese were taken completely unawares and did not begin to fight back for more than an hour later. Those who had been warned to anticipate the trouble expected something similar to the Labour Party's funeral procession (of the preceding Friday) and were prepared to put up shutters and lock themselves in their homes. Even those who were forewarned were taken aback by the savagery of the Malays' attack. They were frightened and panicked.

In Batu Road, Chinese and Indian shopkeepers hurriedly formed themselves into an improvised defence force, using whatever came to hand as weapons. Stones, sticks, iron bars and brickbats were all used, together with kitchen knives, bottles and bamboo poles. Men and boys clambered on to lorries and drove up and down the street, urging non-Malays to unite; groups quickly banded together in a belated attempt to prevent further damage to Chinese property.

Improperly organised, they chased away the invading Malays, who left at the first signs of Chinese resistance. Then, in turn, it was Malay-owned cars and lorries which were smashed and burned by the Chinese. They attempted to burn down the UMNO headquarters, in Batu Road, where two propaganda Land-Rovers had already been set alight. People rushed to the collective protection of

29

their own kind; single individuals were stabbed and beaten by mobs of other races.

The casualties, admitted to the General Hospital that night, give an indication of how the rioting developed. Three senior members of the hospital staff, on duty at the GH, agree that: 'At the outset, between 7 and 8.30 p.m., the first batches of casualties were all Chinese and they were all suffering from parang slashes, stab wounds or mutilations. Between about 8.30 and 10.30 p.m. the casualties, still with slash wounds, contusions or mutilations, were almost equally divided between Chinese and Malays. After about 10.30 p.m. and throughout the night the casualties were almost entirely Chinese and nearly all of them were suffering from gunshot wounds (many sustained at close range with powder burns).'

This same breakdown applies to those who were killed and whose bodies were taken to the General Hospital mortuary. The same hospital authorities say that there were 'about 80 dead by 5 a.m' and they were 'piled, three deep', because of lack of space.

In Batu Road 'the police arrived at about 9 p.m. but did not remain in the area. Later, truck loads of Federal Reserve Units (riot squads) drove past,' one correspondent reported.* 'By midnight the street was almost deserted but sounds of gunfire and the glows of fires showed that trouble had flared up elsewhere.'

A 24-hour curfew, for the whole of Kuala Lumpur, was imposed before 7.30 p.m. and was first announced at 7.35 on the radio. Radio Malaysia continued to announce curfew restrictions and they were repeated on television at 8 p.m. No loudspeaker vans were used; radio and TV alone were used to inform the public, apart from police patrols on the streets who told people to go home.

Many residents, who knew that there was trouble in the area of Princes Road and Kampong Bahru knew nothing at all of the curfew and were shot, by army patrols, late in the evening, many of them in their own gardens or standing in their own doorways. The same journalist continues: 'A number of foreign correspondents saw members of the Royal Malay Regiment firing into Chinese shophouses for no apparent reason. The road itself was completely deserted and no sniping or other violence had been observed (by them).'†

The decision to open fire and 'shoot to kill' was taken by the

* Bob Reece, reporting for the *Far Eastern Economic Review*.
† Bob Reece, reporting for the *Far Eastern Economic Review*.

Inspector General of Police (IGP) Mat Salleh, sometime between 8.30 and 9.0 p.m. This was followed, shortly afterwards, by an order from the Chief of Armed Forces, General Tunku Osman Jiwa, to Malay troops already deployed, telling them also to 'shoot to kill'. While his order was similar to the IGP's it would seem that the Malay troops interpreted the order differently, restricting their targets to Chinese and refraining from shooting at Malays.

Throughout the disturbances there is evidence of considerable friction between the army and the police at all levels. Much of the friction stemmed from the manner in which this original order was interpreted.

Police riot squads were in action in Princes Road early in the evening and, at the beginning, used tear gas in an attempt to control the rioters. It appears that this was the only time when tear gas was used by riot squads. During Phase I there appears to have been no unified control of military and police activity.

In the final analysis the police behaved far more impartially than the army. The Royal Malay Regiment battalions are made up entirely of Malays whereas the Police Force, while predominantly Malay, contains a leavening of Chinese, Indians and Sikhs. Some racial bias was inevitable but the police were concerned with restoring law and order while the Malay troops were concerned with 'teaching the Chinese a lesson'.*

The Sarawak Rangers (from Borneo), who happened to be stationed in the Kuala Lumpur area, were in action on the first night and proved themselves well-disciplined, impartial troops. They were withdrawn, and replaced by Malay troops, after the first thirty-six hours, 'because of their impartiality'.†

*   *   *   *   *

In the absence of any kind of informative announcement by the Government many people listened in to the police radio network, to hear exchanges between police on the ground and police control. Three people whom I met subsequently had the foresight to record some of these exchanges on tape. A great deal can be gained from listening to the tapes now.

* According to a senior officer of 5 Bn the Royal Malay Regiment this same expression was used by a Malay Police Officer when talking of the immediate causes of the riots (p. 19).
† According to the same army officer.

One fact which emerges is that the police in direct contact with the rioters were doing their utmost to take the heat out of the situation; it was police control which was urging them to open fire.

One recorded exchange to which I listened demonstrates this point.

Officer i/c Patrol: 'I need reinforcements. I can control this if I have reinforcements.'

Control: 'How many are you?'

Officer: 'We're five. Only five.'

Control: 'We have nothing to send you. Do the best you can.'

Officer: 'I need more men.'

Control: 'Use your fire weapons. I say again, use your fire weapons.'

(pause)

Officer: 'What about those reinforcements? I can control this if I have more men.'

Control: 'We have nothing to send you. Nothing here available. Use your fire weapons.'

(pause)

Officer: 'This is not easy. What about those reinforcements?'

Control : 'Use your fire weapons! I say again, use your fire weapons!'

Still control, but a different voice: 'God, man! How many more times! I'm giving you a direct order. Use your fire weapons. D'you hear me? Shoot them!'

This exchange was recorded sometime between 9 and 10 p.m. on Tuesday evening (May 13). The exact time is not known, nor, because of the manner in which it was recorded, is it possible to say how long the pauses were, which punctuate the exchange. Nevertheless it appears from this that the man on the ground was doing his best to avoid bloodshed while the police control was not.

All the taped recordings to which I listened were conducted in a mixture of Malay and English. On several occasions when the men on the ground appeared to be under pressure and getting flustered they lapsed into English and the Malay was forgotten. This would indicate that the speakers were non-Malay officers for whom English was their first language.

*　　*　　*　　*　　*

Late on Tuesday night the Prime Minister, Tengku Abdul Rahman, made a radio broadcast in which 'he appealed to all responsible citizens to support and give their fullest co-operation to the security forces in the maintenance of peace and security in the country'.*

It is sad to record that, at a time when some sort of authoritative statement from the Government was needed, the Tengku was completely ineffective. He spoke emotionally and sounded as though he was weeping. He did not tell his listeners what was happening in the city, beyond saying that everything was 'under control'. He concluded his short speech by saying:

'In this hour of need I pray to Allah to secure you against all dangers. At the same time you must look after yourselves. I will do all I can without fear to maintain peace in this country. God bless you all.'*

This did nothing to boost morale. If anything it lowered it.

By this time the situation was quite chaotic; rumour was rife. Many believed, for example, that '2,000 armed Chinese were advancing on Kuala Lumpur from Kepong', which was untrue.

On the same night, Tun Razak (Deputy Prime Minister) and Tan Siew Sin (Chairman of the MCA) also made short broadcast appeals to people to 'stay indoors and remain calm'. No early warning was given before any of these broadcasts and a large percentage of Kuala Lumpur residents did not hear them.

During the first hours of rioting Radio Malaysia issued bulletins which said: 'Do not listen to rumours. The situation is under control.'

Quite clearly it was not. The night sky was bright with the glare of blazing vehicles and burning houses; the bodies of victims were lying in the streets. The continual wail of sirens on police cars, ambulances and fire engines did nothing to give confidence to all those shut indoors, who were literally in terror of their lives. In some parts of town many Chinese spent the night in their homes trying to extinguish burning kerosene rags, flung through smashed windows and splintered shutters by Malay thugs.

People who had been to the evening performance at the Majestic Cinema were caught by the curfew and unable to get home. Police told them to wait in the foyer until transport came. After some delay a police Land-Rover arrived and took away a few of them; the remainder were told to wait for an army lorry.

When the lorry finally arrived, this crowd of impatient people ran out, pushing and scrambling to get into it. The soldier on the

* *Straits Times*: 14 May, 1969.

tailboard of the vehicle, thinking he was being attacked, opened fire on the crowd. Several people were wounded.

A group of Malays, arrested and charged with arson and curfew-breaking, were taken to Campbell Road Police Station. At this time over 2,000 Chinese, mostly from Batu Road, had sought refuge in the police station compound. The police received telephoned orders to release the Malays who were let out of the cells and remained that night in the compound with genuine refugees.

In Lorong Yap Ah Shak (a cul-de-sac on the edge of Kampong Bahru) two elderly Chinese women were forced from their houses by gangs of Malays and killed on their own doorsteps. Hooligans on the pavements shouted: '*China keluar! China keluar!*' ('Chinese out! Chinese out!') and slashed with parangs and knives any who, thinking they knew the Malays well enough to reason with them, opened their doors.

These were the hours of atrocity and bestiality. As I have already said, it is not my intention to record, unnecessarily, stories of atrocities perpetrated during those first twelve hours of rioting. Nevertheless, some mention of them must be made in order to understand the degree of terror to which people were subjected. It explains all the hatred and fear to be found in Malaysia today.

A Chinese woman, alone in her home in Jalan Hale, was unable to prevent rioters from setting her house alight. Burning rags and torches, pushed through half-open louvres, finally set the front rooms ablaze. A Malay woman neighbour called to her through the back door, brought her Malay clothes as a disguise, and led her away to safety through the back garden.

This Chinese woman claimed that several Chinese in Jalan Hale were saved in this way by Malay women neighbours, and that the trouble makers were 'Malays from up-country'. Many other Chinese disagree; they maintain that Chinese shops were destroyed by local Malays who were in debt to Chinese shopkeepers.

A young Chinese courting couple were in a motor car near Circular Road on Tuesday evening. They were surrounded by Malays. The man was dragged out, killed and the car set on fire. At the side of the road, the girl was stripped and her breasts were cut off. She was left for dead, with a broken bottle pushed between her legs. Later she was taken to hospital.

A Chinese was caught at the Golf Club by the curfew; when the curfew was lifted and he was able to return home, he found the dead

34

body of his servant in the garden of his house and, on the doorstep, severed, his mother-in-law's feet. His mother-in-law's body was never found.*

These examples of barbarity could be supported by many similar stories. They are enough to illustrate, with horrid clarity, the primitive behaviour of the Malays who had run amok. Nothing whatsoever can be said to justify this kind of savagery.

A rioting mob of Chinese is equally capable of this kind of behaviour, as any witness to the Singapore riots of 1955 will testify. Chinese rioters can act just as brutally. Any Chinese who question this should be reminded of the immediate post-war massacres, when members of the MPAJA came out of the jungle and put to death literally hundreds of Malays who, rightly or wrongly, they believed had collaborated with the Japanese.

*   *   *   *   *

During Tuesday night, wild rumours circulated by telephone. An effective pronouncement on the radio would have done much to curb them. Telephone switchboards were overloaded; in some districts householders could 'phone out but not receive calls; in others they could receive but not make calls. In some districts the 'phones were working normally; in others they were not working at all.

As the evening wore on Radio Malaysia began to broadcast appeals for blood donors. 'Blood donors are urgently required at the General Hospital.' Anyone who might have contemplated donating blood was curfew-bound, indoors, and too frightened to consider venturing out. 'Curfew breakers will be shot on sight,' continued the radio. The hospital remained short of blood.

It was not until the following day, when the situation at the General Hospital was even more urgent, that blood donors were asked to telephone the hospital, giving their name and address, so that police transport could be sent to collect them.

By 1 a.m. on Wednesday morning there was only one pint of blood left in the General Hospital and they had run out of surgical dressings. Only two qualified surgeons were on duty. A small supply of blood was brought in to them from University Hospital in nearby Petaling Jaya during the night. One member of the staff, commenting on the shortage of blood, said that there was no proper

---

* I have checked and re-checked these stories. I am convinced that they are true.

blood bank and the supply of blood normally kept in the hospital was only sufficient to deal with a serious traffic accident.

* * * * *

Official figures show that 100 lorries, buses and cars were destroyed during the first night and, in addition, a number of motor-cycles and scooters. (In Batu Road alone more than 40 vehicles were burned out.) These figures are, almost certainly, an under-count; but the more serious arson occurred later, during the nights which followed. Most of the 500 houses which were fired were destroyed during Phase II. Officially, only 25 houses and shops were burned in the first night.

There is a great deal of evidence to show that the army was much biased in favour of the Malays during the first night of rioting (and, indeed, during the nights which followed). Police impartiality was regarded by both officers and men of the Malay battalions as an indication of weakness. One Malay army officer told me: 'The police were bloody soft, man!' The troops considered that they were far better qualified to cope with the riots than were the police.

The curfew was rigorously enforced, many say brutally enforced, against the Chinese, while the Malays were allowed to roam the streets at will. Troops manning road blocks chatted and smoked with groups of young Malays while Chinese curfew-breakers were fired upon. A Chinese schoolboy, returning home in a police truck, was taken to within thirty yards of his house and then shot by soldiers as he ran towards his front door. The child was eleven years old; his parents were too frightened to go out to him. His body remained outside the house for the next thirty-six hours—until the curfew was relaxed.*

Foreign journalists saw the army's irresponsible bias and reported it in the world press. Nobody in the Government was able to ensure that the curfew was enforced with equal rigidity against Chinese and Malays.

Ill-disciplined Malay soldiers drove through Chinese streets in jeeps, shooting into ground floor and upstair rooms of Chinese houses. Indoors, people were too frightened to turn on lights or fans since such an indication of their presence could invite gunfire. One elderly Chinese couple described to me how they spent the whole night, sitting up, in the dark, without turning on either the

* Told by the child's relatives.

electric fan or the light. 'Once I searched through a desk drawer with a torch looking for our passports,' the husband said. 'I wanted the passports ready for the morning if we could get away. Even the light from the torch was enough to make them shoot up at the windows.'

His wife said: 'All the time we could hear what we thought was a cat crying. There was nothing we could do. In the morning there was an Indian outside, dead on the pavement.'

Hamzah, the Minister for Information, was quoted as saying that the Malaysian security forces were not involved in any criminal acts, or had seized or looted private property. He said that subversive elements had been masquerading in army-type uniforms to commit various crimes. He assured the public that the security forces had carried out their duties according to law and every complaint against them had been fully investigated.*

At that time, when the whole administration was still disorganised, it seems unlikely that any complaint against the army's behaviour had been investigated. In all probability the Minister had been misinformed.

There is no doubt whatsoever that the Malay soldiers behaved shamefully and yet Government leaders have continued to deny this. Tun Razak is reported as saying: 'The army performed its task very satisfactorily in difficult times. Reports by foreign journalists which give them a bad image were not fair. I emphatically deny that the Malaysian Army acted in any callous way.'†

In fairness to the many Malay civilians who were not responsible for the initial outrages but who later joined in the rioting, it must be said that many false rumours of impending Chinese attack made the Malay men turn out from their kampongs in full force. Rumour bred alarm and confusion; confusion and panic gave rise to further rumour.

Wednesday May 14. Wednesday, after a night of bloodshed and carnage, was comparatively quiet. The enforced curfew kept the Chinese indoors, frightened and apprehensive, while in Malay areas of the city, Malays walked the streets, waiting for Chinese reprisals which never came.

Scores of Malays had, by this time, dressed themselves in black sarongs with a twist of red or white cloth as a headband. This is the traditional garb of a warrior in a holy war. Many people claim that

* *Straits Times*: May 28, 1969.   † *Straits Times*: June 3, 1969.

37

some junior army officers paraded before their men in the same, traditional, makeshift uniform.

During the early hours of Wednesday morning the army made some effort to collect the out-station Malays together and provided transport to send them back to their kampongs. Outside Stadium Negara convoys of army lorries assembled and NCOs shouted out the destination and route to be taken by each lorry; the Malay civilians were loaded on to trucks and driven away from the city and back to their homes.

Wednesday was a quiet day during which Chinese and Malay minorities tried to move to other parts of town; all were concerned with ethnic, geographical groupings.

The three Government stadiums were opened as refugee centres (racially segregated, one for Malays, two for Chinese), and police transport took people either to these centres or to the homes of relatives in other districts. The refugee problem and the work done by the Red Cross and the Civil Defence are discussed later in this account of the disturbances. It is sufficient, at this stage, to realise that small migrations took place on the Wednesday, and that the rioting of the previous night had quietened down.

During these tense hours of waiting, both the Chinese and the Malays expected the other to make the next move. Some fires were still burning; there were further outbreaks of arson as more cars and lorries were set alight, shrill sirens still wailed in the streets but, in contrast to the previous night, Wednesday was quiet.

The whole ugly situation should have been brought under control by noon on Wednesday. With an efficient, centralised Police/ Military Control this would have been possible but the Government had come to a complete standstill. Everybody—Malay, Chinese and Indian—thought that each hour was likely to be his last and reacted, each in his own way. The Tengku, on his own admission, prayed and wept. Many, unknowingly, were following his example. Some, more practical people, packed a few valuables into suitcases and waited for transport to take them away; others spent the day preparing for the next round.

Curfew passes were issued to members of some essential services on Wednesday morning by the police at the High Street Police Station. The passes were valid for twenty-four hours only. One doctor claims that he took $2\frac{1}{2}$ hours to get a pass which he had to renew the following day (Thursday) because initially nobody would authorise

38

the issue of curfew passes for more than twenty-four hours. Subsequently, radio announcements called for all doctors to 'offer their services' and, before doing so, to obtain a curfew pass from the Ministry of Health. The Ministry of Health was not open; applicants who telephoned to Police Headquarters in Bluff Road were told to 'try to get a pass' from High Street Police Station. 'Bluff' is an ironically apt name for the road that accommodates Police Headquarters.

Throughout the day, official releases on Radio Malaysia and on TV continued to say: 'Do not listen to rumour. The situation is under control.' Nothing more informative than this was released.

The Yang di-Pertuan Agong (the Paramount Ruler) issued a proclamation of Emergency on Wednesday. This was announced by the Tengku in his second broadcast on Wednesday night. He spoke of a 'real attempt' by disloyal elements to overthrow the Government by force of arms and spread panic throughout the country.

'The terrorists,' he said, 'under cover of political parties are trying for a comeback.'*

The Emergency was declared in the State of Selangor and certain areas of other States. It was not until the next day that it was extended to cover the whole country.

'My avowed intention,' the Tengku continued, 'is to preserve the country against lawlessness and disorder. . . .

'The Yang di-Pertuan Agong is now empowered to make provision for the apprehension, trial and punishment of persons offending against the regulations.

'He is also enabled to: Make provision for the detention, exclusion and deportation of persons:

'Create offences and prescribe penalties including the death penalty. . . .

'Make special provision in respect of trial, which can even be held in camera. . . .

'. . . . Amend any written law or suspend the operation of any written law, and deprive any person of his citizenship.

'The Government, under the proclamation, may also suspend the elections of the Dewan Ra'ayat and Legislative Assemblies of any State which have not yet been completed.'†

These were indeed far-reaching powers. The references to

* *Straits Times*: May 15, 1969.   † *Straits Times*: May 15, 1969.

deportation of persons and loss of citizenship could however only apply to the Chinese and Indians. A Malay could hardly be deprived of his citizenship; if this happened then to where would he be deported?

The final reference to suspending the elections of the Dewan Ra'ayat (House of Representatives) was the first indication that the elections in Sarawak and Sabah would not be held. The disturbances were still confined to the capital but it was highly probable that the remaining, undecided seats in East Malaysia would all have gone to the Opposition. This was yet a further indication of the Government's fear of the Opposition even though they had a clear working majority, with or without the undecided seats in the Borneo States.

*   *   *   *   *

Leaders of the Opposition parties appealed to the public to co-operate with the Government. Some of them offered to tour the streets with Alliance leaders in an attempt to help restore order. These offers were declined by the Government.

'I have telephoned both the Tengku and Razak,' one Opposition leader said, 'repeatedly suggesting that I go down into the streets to calm my people. But I get no response whatsoever. Meanwhile some of the troops are allowing youths in Malay areas to swagger around carrying knives despite the curfew, but in the Chinese quarters they are standing by while people are burned alive in their houses.'*

Opposition leaders, at the same time, pleaded with the army to take the Malay Regiment away from Chinese areas and replace Malay troops with multi-racial Federal Reserve Units. In particular, the leaders of the moderate Gerakan Ra'ayat offered to help in any way they could. No attempt was made to utilise these offers from Opposition leaders.

Tan Chee Khoon's Gerakan was a party which had received quite considerable support from kampong Malays. In one area near Kuala Lumpur† I talked with many Malay villagers who said: 'During the last two years, Tan Chee Khoon is the only politician who has bothered about us. He's given us medical treatment when we're sick and free medicine when we can't afford to pay. Nobody from UMNO has been near us since the last time they wanted our votes.'

* Dennis Bloodworth, in the *Observer*, May 18, 1969.
† 6th to 8th mile, Demansara Road.

Many of the Malay rioters came from this same area. When I asked them why they had fought against the Chinese during the disturbances, when only a few days earlier they had voted for a multi-racial party, they replied: 'We weren't fighting Tan Chee Khoon. We had to fight the Chinese before they had time to attack us. Thousands were waiting to attack our kampong.'

There were false rumours circulating to this effect at the time and these kampong Malays, several weeks after the event, still believed that their homes were threatened and in danger.

A great deal of good will existed (and still exists) for Tan Chee Khoon of Gerakan and other Opposition leaders but the Government has refused to take advantage of it. It remains untapped. By identifying themselves in any way with the Opposition, Government leaders think they will be admitting failure. The Opposition's valuable contribution continues to be ignored and unacceptable. The Government's failures are plain for all to see.

Two Indian Leaders (both of the Malayan Indian Congress and members of the Alliance), Mr Manickavasagam, Minister of Labour, and Mr Sambanthan, Minister of Works, Posts and Telecoms, both offered to go out into the streets with the police and help in any way they could. Their offers were relayed on the police radio network and were accepted. There was no mention of any similar offers from other Government leaders, who apparently stayed indoors. Armed police escorts were provided for the Tengku, Tun Razak and Tan Siew Sin, between their homes and Radio Malaysia whenever they made a broadcast. At a time when all the Alliance leaders should have been out on the streets many of them were not to be found.

PHASE II—THURSDAY MAY 15–MAY 17

Most of the killing occurred during Phase I of the disturbances (on Tuesday night or in the early hours of Wednesday morning); most of the serious arson—the house burning and the looting—happened during Phase II (on the Thursday night and Friday). The Government was still not in control of the situation, though the army was effectively controlling the Chinese. Malay thugs and, in many instances, Malay troops behaved more or less as they wished.

On Thursday morning there were at least 5,000 refugees in official refugee centres in different parts of town. Most of them were

Chinese; two stadiums were filling up but many more refugees were to arrive there during the next forty-eight hours.

In addition there were several thousand refugees who hàd taken shelter with relatives or friends. The homes of all these people, full of possessions, had been abandoned in a hurry. The majority were Chinese houses on the outskirts of Kampong Bahru or near Jalan Rajah Bot.

These unoccupied houses were systematically looted by Malays and then set alight either on Thursday or Friday. Over 450 houses were destroyed during Phase II. The Malays, after Wednesday's lull, realised that the Chinese were not going to retaliate and, once more, went on the rampage.

Two police inspectors, in uniform, were prevented from entering the area of Kampong Bahru in a police vehicle on Thursday afternoon. At an army road-block a sentry told them: 'You can't enter. The army is in control here!'

They contend that the army was certainly there in some strength but not in control. They report that soldiers in uniform trousers and boots but either bare-chested or wearing civilian shirts, were helping Malay civilians to carry TV sets, radios, reading lamps and household articles from the empty houses. A number of these half-uniformed soldiers wore side-arms or carried weapons.

A score of other people confirm the inspectors' story. One inspector was a Malay, the other was not. The non-Malay described Kampong Bahru that afternoon as: 'Bloody bedlam, with the Malays doing what they liked!' He said this in front of his Malay colleague who did not contradict him.

A subsequent examination of the ruined houses clearly indicated that most of them had been stripped of furniture and fittings before they were set on fire. With the exception of five small burned-down huts, all the destroyed buildings, and I saw many, belonged to Chinese.

Two weeks after the event, when I was taking photographs in the ruins of Lorong Yap Ah Shak, a Malay army sentry challenged me, touching my chest with the tip of his bayonet. He asked me, in Malay, why I was photographing the burned-out houses. I replied that I wanted to have some pictures of these Malay houses which the Chinese had destroyed. This answer satisfied him and, after a short conversation, he allowed me to leave. He confirmed that the houses had belonged to Malays and that the Chinese had burned them down. In fact they were all Chinese houses (36 of them); one had belonged to a Chinese family I used to visit several years ago. On the outskirts of Kuala Lumpur, not far from Circular Road, is Kampong Pandan, another Malay area. Within the Kampong is a single row of shop-houses, newly built. Of these 20 shops, 19 were owned by Chinese and 1 by a Malay. During this period of the disturbances, 19 shops were burned out, individually. The single Malay shop was left untouched.

Also in Kampong Pandan, a Chinese shopkeeper, in a completely separate building, was shut indoors on Thursday night (May 15) when his shop was surrounded by Malays carrying torches. They demanded that he hand over the contents of his shop to them. When he refused to do this they set fire to the shop; he escaped with one child and his wife (who was injured with a parang cut as they ran away). Four other children, still inside, were burned to death. I had no reason to disbelieve this man when he told me his story. He was about 45 years of age; he said: 'I hope I live long enough to kill four Malays.'

* * * * *

During this Phase II period the morale of the Chinese was at its lowest. Leaderless and betrayed, they had nothing but hatred for the Malays and bitterness for the Alliance leaders, unable to regain control.

Tun Razak was named as Director of Operations and the head of a National Operations Council (NOC) on Thursday, May 15, but it was not until the evening of Saturday, May 17, that he announced the members of the Council who would work with him.*

The main function of the NOC was to co-ordinate the work of the Government, the police and the military. Tun Razak explained on the radio that 'full powers have been given to me under the Emergency Regulations—to use fairly but firmly'. At a press conference he said he would handle the situation 'like Templer' and in reply to a question said that the Emergency would go on 'for months and months and months'. Until Saturday evening, however, the National Operations Council existed in name only. This, in itself, was perhaps an indication that Tun Razak was not another Templer.

During this period of hysteria and panic Government spokesmen were quick to blame the disturbances on communist terrorists.

* A list of the members of the National Operations Council is contained in Appendix B.

43

Nobody at all made mention of the fact that these were racial clashes. The Tengku, Tun Razak and Dr Ismail (the ex-Home Minister who rejoined the Government on Thursday) all said that the troubles were communist inspired. In a broadcast (May 17) the Tengku said: 'Last night I blamed the communists alone but intelligence reports say that paid saboteurs were involved too.' He talked of 'evil elements' and 'traitors' and continued: 'There is no going back now. We will fight them hard, hit them really hard to break their backbone and their spirit.'

He said that many Opposition 'workers' had gone to Sabah and Sarawak to create disorder during the elections. 'So, *in order to save the process of democracy*, it is necessary to postpone the elections in those states.'*

These Government allegations, which lumped together the communists and the Opposition parties, only increased Chinese bitterness and despair.

Dr Ismail, in his radio broadcast, said: 'Democracy in Malaysia is dead!' Without any doubt many observers would agree with him, but at the same time question his rider, 'It died at the hands of the Opposition parties.'†

To ignore completely the real causes of the racial conflict and, instead, to raise once again the bogy of communism was criminally stupid. Tun Razak stated that 'Malaysia's image has suffered a serious set-back as a result of the disturbances in Selangor and other parts of the country'. He added that he was confident 'that the communists and other anti-national elements would soon be brought to book'.‡

According to Tun Razak, the Labour Party boycott of the elections had only been a feint. The real strategy of the communists had been to 'intimidate' people into voting for the Opposition. 'The unseen hand of communism,' said Dr Ismail, enlarging on this theme, 'has manoeuvred events, using the Opposition parties as its tools.'¶

All official spokesmen avoided making reference to the fact that the clashes were racial and the Malays were responsible for the aggression.

The 24-hour curfew, imposed on Tuesday evening, was first relaxed briefly on Thursday morning and reimposed quickly when

* *Sunday Times* (of Malaya): May 18, 1969.   † Radio broadcast, May 17, 1969.
‡ At his press conference, May 17, 1969.
¶ The same radio broadcast, May 17, 1969 (footnote †).

further incidents occurred. When the curfew was lifted people who had been stranded in other parts of town for more than thirty-six hours hurried back home; thousands queued outside shops to buy food but, with the first signs of renewed violence, the curfew was again imposed. It was not relaxed on Friday ('mosque-day') but was lifted again on Saturday (May 17) for three hours in the morning.

Again it must be stressed that during the hours of curfew it was the Chinese section of the population that was kept firmly shut up indoors; in the Malay districts of the town Malays moved about the streets at will.

During Phase I and Phase II of these disturbances there was no evidence of any centralised control or organisation. From overheard exchanges on the police radio network it would appear that the city was divided up, arbitrarily, into police areas and army areas. There was no co-ordination.

In conversation with officials afterwards I found that they referred to Police Control, Army Control, Information Control, Special Branch Control and even Joint Control but during the first four days of the disturbances there seems to have been no single co-ordinating body. The Police and the Army were apparently at no time running in harness.

Police helped to move refugees from one part of town to another; the army, with more adequate facilities, helped in moving refugees from army-controlled areas and, by Sunday morning, were providing escorts for Social Welfare workers who helped with food distribution.

Government servants, at home when the troubles started, remained at home and declined to venture into the streets while the curfew was in force. They can hardly be blamed for this. One reason for the breakdown of the Government machinery is that there was no Emergency Control Centre and, even if they were willing to return to duty, officers had no idea what was expected of them nor to where they should report. Constant reminders, on the radio, that curfew-breakers would be shot on sight did little to encourage those who might have been venturesome.

PHASE III—SATURDAY EVENING MAY 17 ONWARDS

After the Deputy Prime Minster, Tun Razak, had announced the formation of his National Operations Council on Saturday evening the first attempts to get the city moving again became apparent.

As Director of the NOC, he had 'supreme powers', Tun Razak told a press conference. He would be responsible to the Tengku, he said, and a multi-racial, emergency cabinet would be formed, 'in a day or two'. He explained: 'There has never been any intention to form an all-Malay cabinet.'* He said that former Home Affairs Minister, Dr Ismail, would also be a cabinet member. Asked if he would seek the co-operation of the Opposition parties in running the Government, Tun Razak replied: 'No, that will not be necessary. We are in control of the country now. We will take responsibility for restoring law and order.'

The NOC would not be superior to the Cabinet, Tun Razak said but 'the Director of Operations (Tun Razak himself) will have powers far above the Ministers'. Tun Razak had emerged as the new leader; for the time being, the Tengku was no longer in the centre of the stage.

On Saturday night, in a radio broadcast, Tan Siew Sin (the only Chinese member of the NOC) announced a Government Plan to 'get supplies moving again, from wholesalers to retailers' (but the small shops were still empty-shelved forty-eight hours later and many people were beginning to go hungry). Throughout the whole period of the disturbances there was, apparently, a more than adequate supply of food in the warehouses. It was only the distribution arrangements which proved unsatisfactory.

The doctor in charge of the General Hospital—an Indian—was quoted as saying: 'The food supply here at GH will run out by tomorrow [Sunday]. The food available will only be sufficient for patients, plus the many discharged patients unable to return home because of the transport shortage.'†

On Sunday the curfew was relaxed from 6.30 to 10 a.m. On Monday it was relaxed still further, from 6.30 a.m. to 12 noon so that the banks could open. This was the first step to stabilising the situation but many Government servants were disinclined to leave their homes and return to work.

On Monday morning radio broadcast appeals for 'all Division I Officers to report for duty as soon as possible'. On Monday afternoon, during curfew hours, this appeal was amended to read: 'Will all Division I Officers report to their offices for duty tomorrow morning at the usual time.' Even though the majority of Division I

* *Straits Times* (Singapore Edition): May 17, 1969.
† *Sunday Times* (of Malaya): May 18, 1969.

46

Officers did return to work on Tuesday many of their juniors did not. Broadcast requests for junior officers were also relayed through the day on Monday and again on Tuesday morning.

When the Kuala Lumpur curfew was lifted, on Monday morning, it still remained in force in the area of Kampong Bahru and at Kampong Pandan; here, the 24-hour curfew was retained. Since, in Malaysia, 'Chinese' and 'communist' are often thought to be synonymous by Government leaders and, in view of the Alliance insistence that this trouble was communist-inspired, it is significant that the Kampong Bahru and Pandan districts are predominantly Malay and that any Chinese who had lived there before were now taking refuge elsewhere.

Kampong Bahru continued to remain the head-quarters of an extremist group of Malay religious fanatics who called themselves Komandos Al Allah (The Commandos of God). Racists, only too ready to resort to violence, they were not suppressed but were for the time being contained within the Kampong area.

The curfew restrictions were gradually relaxed, during the days that followed. By the end of the month the curfew was enforced from 3 in the afternoon until 6.30 the next morning. On Friday, May 30, the Information Control Centre announced that 'the curfew cannot be relaxed further at the moment as feelings are still running high. The Tengku fears that ill-feelings will spread to the class-rooms.'*

'If this happened,' the Tengku is reported as saying, 'then the children of this country would grow up to hate one another.'

Many people commented on the naïveté of the Tengku's statement. One responsible citizen said: 'Chinese school children have been killed by the Malays, had their schools and homes burned down by Malays, seen their parents killed or arrested by Malays, gone hungry because of the Malays. There will always be hatred in the classrooms now. Always.'

Casualty Figures. The official Government figures for the number of killed during the first few days of the rioting was 178. This undoubtedly is an underestimate.

Obviously the exact numbers of dead will never be known but even a conservative estimate puts the figure at over 800. Some foreign observers and correspondents suggest that the number goes into four figures, and this is possible; rumour in Kuala Lumpur and

* *Straits Times*: May 30, 1969.

47

Singapore had it that 'at least 2,500 died', and this, without doubt, is an exaggeration.

Officially, more than six hundred people are still missing, but, according to unofficial Social Welfare and Police sources, those still unaccounted for since the disturbances started are more than 800. Even supposing that a percentage of these has returned home without telling the authorities, there is still a considerable number of people missing.

Assuming that as many as 200 of those reported missing have returned to their families it means that some 600, still untraced, can be added to the official figure of 178. There are presumably still more who are missing and have never been reported as missing. At a very rough estimate some 800 people were killed during the first week of racial violence.

Some bodies were thrown into the Klang river; one Malay Government servant told me that he had counted 'ten or twelve' floating past his house. There is no indication that any dead are still left in the ruins of burned out houses, despite contradictory rumour.

One confusing factor is that police officers (Inspectors and senior ranks) were authorised to bury bodies wherever they found them, or dispose of them as best they could. 'Inquests and inquiries can be dispensed with. Proper documentation should be made, however, before the disposal of these bodies.'* 'But documentation was quite impossible,' one police officer told me. 'Most of these corpses had been two or three days in the sun. Some of them fell to pieces when we tried to pick them up. Others had been slashed and mutilated when they were killed. Nobody wanted to go through their pockets, trying to identify them.'

This is a sickening comment, but it indicates the difficulty of trying to estimate the number of people killed. The deep tin-mining pools, in the bare arid land on the outskirts of the city, probably still hide a few bodies more. The exact numbers of dead will never be known.

At the Sungei Buloh leper settlement, fifteen miles north of Kuala Lumpur, over a hundred bodies were buried in a mass grave. In their hurry to bury the dead, the authorities were singularly unimaginative in their choice of a grave site. All Asian peoples hold strong views about the contagion of leprosy. During the Festival of Ching Ming, when Chinese annually worship at family graves,

* *Straits Times*: May 21, 1969.

48

nobody will care to visit a mass grave in a leper settlement. But they will remember; and the Ching Ming festival will serve as an annual reminder of these days of bloodshed and massacre.

In case any Government officials should ever deny that such a mass burial took place, it can be stressed that the whole macabre happening was filmed, at the time, and within days shown outside Malaysia, on television in Asian countries. The lorries, the police, the grave-diggers, the bulldozer, the settlement signboard, and the pathetic mounds of dead, were all recorded on film together with a final sequence, showing a man with a rake, collecting together odd shoes, a slipper, a handbag and a piece of clothing. He made a small bonfire of them on the broken earth, perhaps without realising the camera was filming him.

Refugee Centres: Welfare Work: Food Distribution. The racial bias shown by Malay soldiers who were supposed to enforce the curfew was evidenced again by army and welfare services responsible for the distribution of food and relief supplies. In refugee centres, and in isolated communities, the Malays were better cared for and received better treatment than the Chinese.

Refugee centres were opened at three Government Stadiums and at several schools during the first night of the rioting. The Red Cross Headquarters had only three ambulances (one broken down), two mini-buses and one car but nevertheless did its best to establish these centres and keep them functioning until the Civil Defence Services were able to take them over. At the beginning they were not only short of transport, but also of food, blankets, stoves and other essentials.

On Thursday morning (May 15) there were:

3,000 Chinese refugees in Merdeka Stadium
1,200 Chinese refugees in Chinwoo Stadium
700 Chinese refugees in Shaw Road School
650 Malay refugees in Stadium Negara

On Sunday morning (May 18):

Chinese in Merdeka Stadium had increased to 3,500
Chinese in Chinwoo Stadium had increased to 1,500
Chinese in Shaw Road School had increased to 800
Malays in Stadium Negara had *decreased* to 250

The maximum number of refugees being housed and cared for by the Red Cross and the Civil Defence Services in all centres was not

49

more than 8,000. But, as these figures show, the number of Chinese refugees increased with each day of the disturbances while the number of Malay refugees decreased.

Singapore's Chinese Chamber of Commerce donated M$500,000 to a Relief Fund. In addition it despatched a large quantity of food parcels, clothing, blankets and cigarettes. The Tengku ordered that all the Relief Fund money (and donations in kind) be administered by the Ministry of Social Welfare.

In Kuala Lumpur itself, as I have already mentioned, there was sufficient food but the distribution methods were unsatisfactory. A large amount of food was stockpiled at Jalan Hishamuddin School but there was not sufficient transport available to get this moving. A large provision store in Mountbatten Road was running out of stock by Monday morning (May 19), thirty-six hours after Tan Siew Sin had announced his plan to keep retailers supplied.

In outlying districts and on the outskirts of Kuala Lumpur the food shortage was more acute. An official who visited the Sungei Way area (a few miles outside the capital) on Sunday morning found Chinese villages displaying signboards which said: 'SOS MUKANAN PERLU' (i.e. 'Desperate for Food'). Chinese foodshops had not been restocked since the previous Tuesday and people here were starving.

In one Chinese settlement (near Sungei Way) the people had nothing to eat except tapioca roots. They were only a few hundred yards from a Malay kampong where cases of food were stacked underneath the houses, guarded by soldiers.

The Civil Defence Services took over the refugee centre at the Merdeka Stadium from the Red Cross on Wednesday afternoon (May 14). At that time there were 1,006 Chinese already there. This number had increased to 3,528 by Saturday afternoon (May 17). For the first forty-eight hours food was short but there was sufficient rice. The main problems were toilet facilities, a shortage of blankets and an inadequate water supply. Initially there was only one cooker. The Red Cross had produced 190 blankets and later the army brought another 250. These had to be shared between 3,500 but many had been able to bring blankets, small cooking stoves, pots and pans with them. The CDS borrowed 4 more cookers on Friday.

Two CDS officers told me that they organised relief for their own centre since no adequate assistance came from the Government. They were never without a telephone and were able to arrange for donations of rice, dried fish and vegetables to be sent in by Chinese (many of whom made anonymous donations). These gifts did not begin to reach them till the relaxation of the curfew on Saturday morning (May 17).

None of the parcels from Singapore's Chinese Chamber of Commerce reached them. They were promised a consignment of four army truckloads of tinned Nestlé products by Social Welfare but, though the army accepted these for delivery, they never arrived. (One Police Officer claims to have seen Malay soldiers in Jalan Hale tearing the CCC gift labels from food parcels and giving them to Malays. It was apparently necessary to remove the labels since devout Muslims might otherwise have felt disinclined to eat Chinese food.)

Among the Merdeka Stadium refugees was a high percentage of small children and babies. Powdered milk was in short supply. The CDS officers said that a telephone call was made to the manager of a European commercial firm, 'to beg him for tins of powdered milk'. The manager appeared somewhat surprised at this request and said that he had already donated his entire stock (of 30,000 tins) to the Relief Fund. Not one of these tins reached the refugees in the Merdeka Stadium. Later, on Monday, the manager sent eighteen tins in his own car, with a scribbled note saying that this was all he had managed to scrape together.

Understandably, there was a shortage of tobacco and packets of cigarettes were being used for barter. On June 16, one month after the disturbances, I was talking with a Malay officer from the Social Welfare Ministry. He offered me a Benson and Hedges cigarette saying: 'Take one, lah! These are free issue. We all received a carton a day, while we were doing emergency relief work. I haven't smoked all mine yet!'

One month after the rioting there were still over 1,000 refugees left in the Merdeka Stadium. They had received nothing from the Relief Fund and were being maintained by Social Welfare grant at eighty cents per head, daily.

Many were waiting for accommodation and refused to go back to areas where the Malays predominated. Most of them owned little apart from the clothes they were dressed in. One man said that he used to own a well-stocked farm. His livestock was all stolen, he maintained, by soldiers with lorries during Thursday and Friday (May 15 and 16); they then burned down his house, his cowshed, his car and his tractor. His total possessions, when he spoke to me, were worth less than $20.

THE GOVERNMENT AND THE PRESS

The Minister of Information and Broadcasting, Senu bin Abdul Rahman (of UMNO), was beaten in the elections and lost his seat to the Pan Malayan Islamic Party. His successor, Hamzah bin Dato Samah (Tun Razak's brother-in-law) assumed office only after the disturbances had started. This meant that the Information Services began at a disadvantage but the Alliance Government's information machinery has always been lacking in horse-power; there is no reason to suppose that, with Senu still holding the reins, the information pony-cart would have moved forward any more smoothly.

The riots began after office hours, so, from the outset, there was nobody in the ministry able to take charge; there was no skeletal staff to provide any sort of emergency service. Despite the long history of racial friction in Malaya, the Information Services were completely unprepared for what happened and had no contingency plans ready. From the very beginning they failed to keep the public informed. Since Government ministers also were uninformative one must suppose that it was Government policy to remain silent.

Because of the curfew, most of Kuala Lumpur was without newspapers from Wednesday morning until Sunday. There was no distribution on Wednesday or Thursday, either in the capital or outside to the rest of the country. On Friday and Saturday a total censorship ban was imposed and no newspapers were published. On Sunday morning (May 18) for the first time for five days, people were able to buy a paper during the three-hour curfew break. Many shoppers were in a hurry to get back home and did not bother to look for a paper; they had to wait till Monday before they had any news to read.

During the whole of this period there was no proper news release issued by a Government spokesman and no Government emergency newsheet or hand-out was published. Members of the public only knew what they gathered from ministers' broadcasts—that communist-terrorists had attempted to take over and that the Government had assumed strong emergency powers to deal with the situation. Unsure of what was happening in the country it is not surprising that

52

people listened to police radio calls; those with short-wave receivers listened to the World Programme of the BBC, which is easy to receive in Malaysia.

Hamzah, at one press conference, said that he was now Minister of Information and all correspondents were free to phone him personally at any hour of the day or night. He would be only too pleased to reply to their queries, he told them. From then on he was unable to answer any questions at all and finally one journalist asked: 'What's the point of giving us your phone numbers if you can't tell us anything?'

At another press briefing a collection of captured weapons was produced and shown to correspondents. These, it was alleged, were captured communist arms and proof of communist involvement. The 'weapons' were spears, tridents and ceremonial axes with bamboo handles. One correspondent,* with many years of Asian experience, commented that they looked like hand props from a Chinese opera. An angry official grabbed hold of a rusty spear and banged it on the floor shouting, 'That's no hand prop!' He may have been right, but at such times of rioting and insecurity a broken bottle could be called an offensive weapon.

At these press briefings tempers flared and voices were raised. Hamzah, Tun Razak and officials from the Information Control Centre all managed to antagonise the foreign press, nevertheless the overseas reporting was fair and objective. When Hamzah denied that there was any truth in allegations that the army was biased and ill-disciplined one newsman demanded: 'Are we to report what you tell us or what we see with our own eyes?'

On Thursday afternoon, when the local press was suspended until censorship regulations could be drawn up, Hoffman, the Editor-in-Chief of the *Straits Times* made a strong plea against these official moves.† He remarked to Hamzah that only Malaysians were prevented from finding out what was going on. Hamzah replied that the ban was necessary because of the inflammatory articles printed in the local press, before and during the elections. To this Hoffman protested: 'Is a civil servant going to tell me what is inflammatory and what is not?'‡

* Mark Gayn, of the *Toronto Star.*
† Tan Sri Hoffman's plea against official censorship moves carried great weight not only because of the standing of his newspaper but because of his own reputation—especially for courage during the war against Japan.
‡ *Far Eastern Economic Review*: May 22, 1969.

In a later editorial the *Straits Times* said that the widest possible powers of censorship had been given to the Minister of Home Affairs. These it considered unnecessary. The editorial referred to the 'horrifying thought' that a police inspector 'who might dislike what we have written here, will be able, on and after the appointed day, to arrest it'.

On Saturday—after an angry exchange at the previous day's press briefing—some foreign correspondents had their curfew passes withdrawn, 'for their own safety'. Eventually journalists were not allowed to move about freely and had to ask for a police escort if they wanted to leave their hotels.

On Monday (May 19) foreign correspondents were given official transport from their hotels to the Information Control Centre and asked to bring their typewriters with them. After the briefing they were invited to write their stories, then and there, and hand them in for cabling. From Monday onwards the foreign press was kept on a tighter rein.

In view of the Tengku's announcement that, in the course of time, he will compile a true picture of events, which will counter the false descriptions the foreign press projected, it is of some significance to re-read exactly what the foreign press reported which gave such offence.

Foreign journalists have been strongly criticised by the Alliance Government. Malay leaders have been particularly sensitive about allegations of the army's racial bias (and yet this can be proved beyond all doubt). The suggestion that the Alliance had shown itself unable to co-exist with any opposition is also a matter about which they are sensitive. Malay leaders have insisted, over and over again, that journalists 'did not give a true picture of events', that their reporting was 'distorted' and their political comment was 'irresponsible' and 'unfair'.*

The opposite of this is true. The reporting and the political comment was accurate and fair. *Time* magazine and *Newsweek*—whose issues were banned by the police Special Branch—both gave factual accounts of the disturbances as they occurred. The *Far Eastern Economic Review*, in another banned issue, gave a balanced,

* The only dissenting view was expressed in an article by Derek Davies, published in the *Far Eastern Economic Review* on June 26. Referring to himself as 'a slower pressman who came to evaluate the aftermath,' Mr Davies labelled earlier correspondents as 'professional vultures' and concluded that an overly pessimistic picture of the situation had been painted in the foreign press.

carefully considered report. British journalists, and in particular Fred Emery of *The Times*, who was singled out for criticism, were at no time filing exaggerated stories. Yet all of Fred Emery's published pieces were censored at Subang airport; *The Times* too, was banned.

At Subang, outside Kuala Lumpur, issues of all these publications I have mentioned, together with copies of the *Daily Telegraph*, the *Sunday Times*, the *Observer*, the *Financial Times*, *The Economist*, and some Australian newspapers, were confiscated and burned by the censor.

A cursory examination of the content of some of these papers explains why they were unacceptable to the Government but their comment is none the less valid. It is difficult to see how any honest commentary on the riots could fail to upset the Malaysian Government at such a moment.

In London, *The Times* said: 'Blaming trouble on the communists —as the Malaysian Government has so readily done this week—will not bring the responses it used to do.' Also: 'If any slender links do remain with the racial harmony of the past they will have to be tended and strengthened with much more skill and imagination than the Government in Kuala Lumpur has shown this past week.'

The *Economic Review*, in an editorial, said: 'Kuala Lumpur, swept by mob violence, seemed to symbolise Malaysia's death wish, a horrid act of communal suicide.'

Dennis Bloodworth, writing in the *Observer*, likened the Government's endeavour to restore peace to a man trying to muzzle a bull with a red rag.

The Economist said: ' . . the National Operations Council appears more and more to be sweeping the storm water off the decks while the sea pours in where the keel used to be.'

'From now on stability in Malaysia will depend on the riot police as much if not more than the politicians . . . the main question is whether any chances remain of arresting the drift towards chaos and confusion.' (The *Financial Times*.)

'Official [casualty] figures and pronouncements bear little relation to the real facts, which are very grisly indeed.' (*The Economist*.)

Harvey Stockwin, in the Australian *Bulletin* asked: 'How to write objectively about a governing elite which insists upon behaving as if it had something to hide and which, armed ten times over with power over every life and limb in the country, seemingly refuses to see the essential truth that you ... cannot suppress all the people all the time? It has castrated its own press, assaulted its own credibility and needlessly alienated the world press.'

Ian Ward's final comment, in an article published in the *Daily Telegraph*, summed it all up quite simply. 'The Malaysian race war,' he wrote, 'has added a whole new dimension to South-east Asian politics.'

Though issues of many British and American newspapers and periodicals were banned in Malaysia, they were, of course, for sale on the book stalls of Singapore. Photostat copies of the articles they contained about Malaysia were soon smuggled across the causeway and being passed from hand to hand in Kuala Lumpur. In particular, Fred Emery's articles in *The Times* were much sought after. A random selection of five or six articles was selling for M$20 during the first week of June. These photostats were declared to be subversive and, for some people, possession of them resulted in arrest and imprisonment.

It is a distressing comment on Malaysia today that people are now in detention because they were found to have a clipping from *The Times*.

The efforts of the Government and the National Operations Council to restore peace do not include a noticeable contribution from the Ministry of Information. While Radio Malaysia broadcast warnings that people should not listen to rumour, and announced that the penalties for rumour-mongering were a M$1,500 fine or twelve months' imprisonment, or both, no attempt was made to counter the rumours or release factual accounts of what was happening in the city.

The errors made by the Information Services were glaring and frequent.

The Tengku, Tun Razak and Dr Ismail, when they made radio broadcasts, spoke in English or Malay. Summaries of their speeches were re-broadcast in Chinese (Mandarin) but no government official made a broadcast in Chinese. Tan Siew Sin, President of the Malayan Chinese Association and Chairman of the (Chinese) Hokkien Association, cannot speak any Chinese language or dialect and broadcast only in English.

Kuala Lumpur is a predominantly Cantonese city; it is remarkable that throughout the period of the disturbances Chinese radio announcements were made in Mandarin (unless broadcast to 'the minorities' which have limited radio time). From Government, no Chinese face, speaking Chinese, appeared on the TV screen. Not one member of the National Operations Council can speak Chinese.*

No more than five minutes warning was given before a Government leader made a TV or radio broadcast, with the result that many people did not hear them.

One of the most effective speeches was made by the Yang di-Pertuan Agong (the Paramount Ruler) on June 4, his official birthday. He spoke wisely on the need to preserve multi-racial harmony and was the first to offer condolences to the relatives of those killed in the riots. His speech, in Malay, was followed at once by an English translation. Here again radio listeners were given only five minutes advance warning before his broadcast began ; many did not hear it, yet the Information Ministry presumably knew well in advance that the Paramount Ruler's birthday was approaching and that he would broadcast to the nation.

Some of the rumours which were circulating in Kuala Lumpur were so obviously untrue that, clearly, there was no need to deny them. One old woman told me that the dead bodies of 'hundreds of Chinese' had been taken in lorries to the East Coast, 'to show the Malays there that mainly Malays had been killed'. Apparently, the dead were painted with tar so that they should not be recognised as Chinese. This kind of nonsense was told and re-told; many believed it. Lack of reliable information meant that rumours became more horrific with the re-telling.

The Information Control Centre† was a bottleneck through which information did not pass. As an example, a typical ICC release would report: 'The situation in the Kuala Lumpur area remains tense. There will be no relaxation in the curfew restrictions for the time being. Only two incidents have been reported, during the last 24 hours.'

No details of 'the incidents' would be given. Gossip and rumour thrived on this. New stories of death and destruction would conclude with 'those are the two incidents they mentioned on the radio this morning'. The incidents were probably of little significance but,

* *Vide* Appendix B.
† This was later re-named and is now called the Information Co-ordination Centre.

57

in the absence of fact from the ICC, rumours and fiction flourished.

One false rumour, which was given general credence, asserted that the main water supply for the capital had been poisoned and that tap-water was not fit to drink. The Information Services made no effort to counter this at all but merely reiterated that the public should not listen to rumour.

Two reporters from a local paper telephoned the Information Control Centre to confirm an item of news. On the basis of this press query they were accused of rumour-mongering and arrested.

It was extremely difficult for the Alliance Information Ministry to prevent the spread of rumour. Whatever they had done would have left them open to criticism. The fact that they did nothing makes it hard to sympathise with them but much of the rumour was in fact accurate. For example: A Chinese woman doctor, driving a car, saw a Malay at the side of the road, apparently injured. She stopped and went to help him. The man leapt to his feet, waving a parang and decapitated her. This ugly rumour was a true story. In this case, there was little the Information Services could do except insist that the public should not spread rumours and repeat that there were heavy penalties for doing so.

They made no attempt to refute false rumour or issue factual information. They were confronted by a succession of dilemmas, and they did nothing. With no newspapers for several days, total censorship for forty-eight hours and no official Government news sheets, the public was indeed poorly served by its Ministry of Information.

AFTERWARDS

THE FOLLOWING MONTHS

In this account of the Kuala Lumpur disturbances I have tried, as objectively as possible, to record not only a detailed description of the riots themselves but an explanation of the causes which led to them.

Rioting mobs of Malays and Chinese are both capable of barbarous behaviour. The great tragedy of May 1969 was that the authorities gave protection to one racial group only and the rioters were suppressed on the basis of race. With a rigidly enforced curfew, force and determination, the violence could have been controlled within the first twenty-four hours. Instead it lasted for several days, with a senseless loss of life and destruction of buildings and property.

In an attempt to explain the apparent irresponsibility of the Malay soldiers it could be said that they received no clear directives from above. The threat to Malaysia's internal security has been posed by Chinese communists for many years. It is understandable that they might have jumped to the wrong conclusions in the heat of the moment, when they saw Malays chasing Chinese through the streets. But this does not excuse the breakdown of discipline which followed.

During the rioting the Malays lost their sense of reason and judgement. The Government overreacted and made serious errors which it will be difficult for them to rectify. The State of Emergency has established what is, in effect, Malay rule by decree through the National Operations Council.

An understanding of the causes of the May troubles makes it clear that the present course of action being followed by the NOC will not restore Chinese confidence nor even a façade of racial harmony. It can do nothing but harm to the country; further rioting and conflict will be the inevitable outcome.

No political party has gained anything at all as a result of these disturbances, except the Malayan Communist Party (MCP) which has gained considerably.

THE PROSPECT OF COMMUNIST SUBVERSION

The attempts of the Malay leaders to blame communist-terrorists for the disturbances were not convincing; after their initial hysteria they appeared unconvinced themselves. Yet several thousand people, mostly Chinese have been arrested; included in their numbers are newly-elected Opposition Members of Parliament and State Assemblymen.

Though the Government modified its original accusations of communist aggression it has still continued to blame the Opposition Parties for the disturbances and refused to acknowledge Malay complicity. The views which some senior members of UMNO express in private differ considerably from the official line. One UMNO minister, who wished to remain anonymous, said, 'Without doubt some young Malay hot-heads were responsible. But these are youngsters who are difficult to control.'

It is this inability of the UMNO moderates to control their extremists which is of such concern at the moment.

The Chinese community knows only too well to what extent these 'young Malay hot-heads' were responsible. The Chinese are now seriously alarmed at the Government's intention of raising nine new battalions for the army and the Police Field Force, since they realise that the new recruits must come from the ranks of these Malay 'youngsters who are difficult to control'. Having seen how they can behave as civilians, armed only with spears and parangs, they find the prospect of them being trained and armed with automatic weapons, at best, depressing.

Britain, Australia and India have been asked to provide the weapons necessary to equip these new units. A number of Chinese, from all sections of the community, said to me: 'Surely England isn't going to supply machine-guns and rifles to these people—when we have nothing whatsoever to protect ourselves with?'

While the present Government in Malaysia is fully aware of the extreme dangers of racial polarisation it is difficult to see how they can prevent it if they continue on their present course. The situation cannot be improved by introducing more and more stringent emergency powers, or by damping down the heat of racial tensions with layer upon layer of force. No Malay leader will go out into the streets and move among the people unless accompanied by bodyguards with sten-guns; the Malay leadership is utterly out of touch with Chinese feeling. By reassuring the Chinese, the National Operations Council will antagonise the Malay extremists who are demanding a one-race Government. The only Chinese in the NOC is Tan Siew Sin, who is now discredited in the eyes of both the Chinese community and a large percentage of the Malays.

The young Chinese, who have been keen to participate in the political life of the country, now find themselves leaderless and unprotected. It is inevitable that they will begin to band themselves together and look elsewhere for support. They are now susceptible to communist propaganda and only too ready to join communist front or clandestine organisations. Many Labour Party members have been arrested. Those with communist views, who are still at large, now have a propaganda seed-bed already prepared for them by Malay ineptitude and racialism. No underground propaganda teams can ever before have had their task made so easy.

The ten-year-old remnants of the communist guerrilla force, in semi-hibernation on the Thai border, are unlikely to benefit from this state of affairs as long as they remain where they are. In May they were as unprepared as the Malaysians and taken unawares by the disturbances. They will need to come south and re-establish their old lines of communication and supply. (Their probing, reconnaissance patrols are only just beginning.) Once this has been accomplished there is no reason at all why the same kind of Emergency that Malaya knew in the 1950s should not develop. Malay troops (as their record in Sarawak and Sabah during the time of Indonesian confrontation showed) have neither the stamina nor discipline needed for jungle combat. It took the British Army (aided by Gurkhas, Australians and New Zealanders) twelve years to put down the first Emergency. Malay battalions on their own would find the task of containing a second one far beyond their capabilities.

Two Chinese boys (aged 17 and 18) told me, early in June, that it was too soon for them to go into the jungle. 'There are no fighters for us to join up with,' one said, 'but we'll go at the proper time.'

I do not believe that these two Chinese youngsters were expressing a romantic, minority view. Many Chinese youths think and feel as they do. 'Vietnam isn't far from Malaya,' is a commonly expressed thought. 'We'll get our weapons when the Americans have gone home.'

One Opposition politician told me that he knew 'for certain, that many Chinese have gone north, to join the communists in Thailand'. There was no way of confirming this statement. It is likely that some may have gone by now but talk of 'many' seems an exaggeration.

Peking's reaction to the May disturbances, though slow in coming, was predictable. Initially no mention was made of racial conflict, but the troubles were blamed on the 'Rahman-Razak puppet clique, lackey of US-British Imperialism'. It was not until August 9 that the *New China News Agency* issued a statement from the Central Committee of the Communist Party of Malaya. This claimed that '3,000 innocent people have been killed by the enemy's guns and knives. Ninety per cent of those who lost their lives were of Chinese nationality.' The Malayan National Liberation Army was growing, it maintained; guerrilla zones were being consolidated and expanded. It called on people of all nationalities to join together in opposing the present Government. This kind of exaggerated propaganda was to be expected; it will have an immediate appeal to young Malayan Chinese searching for political expression.

JUNE 28
During the period of appraisal and assessment which followed the May riots one further incident occurred, at the end of June, which was as significant as the May disturbances themselves.

More rioting broke out on June 28. I mention it here, rather than refer to it in the main account of the rioting, for two reasons. Firstly, it was a completely separate incident which happened five weeks after the race-riots began; secondly, it occurred because the National Operations Council was so preoccupied with the dangers of communist subversion (which I have just described) that it failed to contain the Malay extremists responsible for the original outbreak. In the wake of the rioting, 'communist-terrorists' were arrested; several thousand 'troublemakers' and 'bad elements' (mostly Chinese) were detained, but the Malay ultra-nationalists were not even publicly reprimanded.

On June 28, when the rioting began again, for the first time it was the Indians who were attacked and not the Chinese. In Sentul, a Malay suburb of Kuala Lumpur, fifteen Indians were slashed to death and several others injured. Chinese squatter huts were burned down and, by midnight, over seventy Indians and Chinese had moved to a refugee centre. These figures are small when compared with the numbers that were killed five weeks earlier but the young Malays who were responsible had a new slogan. 'We've finished with the pigs! Now for the goats!' they shouted as they attacked the Indians in Sentul.

In mid-May the Chinese had borne the brunt of the Malay

attack. The Indian community, though sympathetic, had remained on the fence and done its best not to get involved. After June 28 the Indians were committed and they had no option but to come down on the Chinese side. With one act of lunacy the Malay extremists alienated the entire Indian community, Hindus and Muslims alike.

Again, as previously, rumours were rife and the Information Co-ordination Centre (ICC) did nothing to dispel the fears of the public. At 11 p.m. Radio Malaysia announced that 'some incidents and cases of arson had occurred in Selangor' but, for more than three hours before this, Kuala Lumpur residents had heard the sound of gunfire and seen the glow of burning buildings.

Even the co-operative *Straits Times* became impatient with the ICC's incompetence. In an editorial headed 'Information Please' it asked: 'Would citizens' nerves not have been steadied and rumour throttled by honest news quickly given over radio and television? And would not credibility have been restored, and assurance believed, had the newspapers been able to publish a sober, factual account for the breakfast table?'

Where the ICC is the only recognised source of news, and strict censorship powers are enforced, it is almost impossible for the *Straits Times* or any other local newspaper to function usefully.

As a result of this incident, racial antagonism between Malays and non-Malays has become worse than at any other time in the country's history.

PRESENT AND FUTURE

ONE-PARTY RULE AND THE ULTRA-NATIONALISTS

The immediate prospects for multi-racial co-operation are bleak. The present UMNO leaders cannot risk offending the Malays for fear of widening the rift within their own party. They are well aware of the dangers of one-party rule but they have left themselves little room to manoeuvre. There is only one road open to them which might lead to success. While placating the Malays, and retaining Malay support, they must allow the Chinese some measure of political expression, even if this means encouraging an Opposition to emerge. This may be an impossible task. If the Tengku is able to hold his party (UMNO) together and if the Malayan Chinese Association and the moderate Gerakan Ra'ayat can be persuaded to co-operate, then Malaysia might still have a democratic future. As long as the Opposition is suppressed there can be no long-term solution to the country's difficulties.

Tun Razak told one correspondent* that the policy of the National Operations Council was to 'do nothing' but ensure the preservation of law and order, and wait, hoping that tensions would relax and memories fade. A continued policy of 'do nothing' at the present time will prove fatal to any chances of Malaysian recovery. Parliament cannot meet yet, Tun Razak insists, because public debate of racial issues will heighten tension. When it does finally meet there will be 'certain things' that cannot be said and freedom will be 'within limits'.†

Tan Siew Sin, President of the Malayan Chinese Association and the only Chinese member of the NOC, claimed that 'a premature return to parliamentary democracy could produce a bigger racial bloodbath in Malaysia than the riots of May 13. Certain rules will have to be changed,' he said, 'before parliamentary rule can return.

'Parliamentary democracy can only succeed if the areas of agreement between the Government and the Opposition are 85 per cent, but the area of agreement is only 15 per cent,' he maintained.

'In fact, in this country, the Government and the Opposition

* *Far Eastern Economic Review*: July 10, 1969.
† UPI report: Kuala Lumpur, August 15, 1969.

disagrees on vital, fundamental issues, and a premature return to democracy can only lead to disaster for the whole country.'*

It is not difficult to appreciate why Tan Siew Sin no longer commands the respect of the Malaysian Chinese. He, too, is supporting the NOC policy of 'do nothing'.

The Tengku is being made to walk a very slender tightrope. When complete power passed to Tun Razak many observers assumed that the Tengku's political eclipse had begun. 'I give the instructions,' the Tengku said, 'but I cannot be chairman of the National Operations Council because there is a lot of work involved. I have got to think of the bigger things.'†

For two months the Tengku was in semi-retirement. There was apparently no question of Tun Razak replacing him; the father-and-son relationship between the Prime Minister and his Deputy was maintained. The Tengku went into hospital for an eye operation, long overdue, and then took a convalescent holiday in Port Dickson. As Director of Operations, Tun Razak continued to run the NOC, with its negative policy of 'do nothing'.

The Tengku's return to politics precipitated another crisis, bringing all the dissensions within the United Malay National Organisation (UMNO) out into the open.

A little known UMNO backbencher, Dr Mahathir bin Muhammed, wrote a letter to the Prime Minister which, politely phrased in 'Rajah Malay', demanded his resignation. This letter found its way into the press and was immediately banned. Angrily the Tengku dismissed Mahathir from the Party's central executive committee. (Had an Opposition backbencher written such a letter he would undoubtedly have found himself in detention without delay.)

Before dismissal, Mahathir attended an UMNO meeting to give account of himself. He presented a petition, signed by Malay University students, which supported his letter and demanded the Tengku's resignation.

In Kuala Lumpur on July 17 more than 1,500 Malay students demonstrated on the University campus, demanding that 'The Tengku must go!' Chanting anti-Tengku slogans, they burnt an effigy which depicted him as a senile anglophile. 'When are you going to pay homage to the Queen again, Tengku?' they shouted, and 'Aren't the British going to miss you?'

* Reuter report: Kuala Lumpur, August 4, 1969.
† In an interview with *The Times* correspondent: May 20, 1969.

In the meantime copies of Mahathir's banned letter continued to circulate throughout the country.

A University lecturer, Mukhtaruddin Dazin, published a leaflet which was distributed to all Malays attending the National Mosque for prayers on July 4. This, too, was classified as inflammatory and banned.

The views expressed in these two publications are not simply those held by two individuals on the lunatic fringe of Malaysian politics. They are views held by a great number of Malays in the country. For this reason it is worth considering what they have to say.

'You have always compromised by giving in to the Chinese,' Mahathir allegedly wrote to the Prime Minister. 'The Chinese look upon you and the Alliance Government as cowards and weaklings. Consequently they are no longer afraid to reject the Alliance; the Malays, on their part, no longer desire the Alliance. It is for this reason that the Chinese and Indians showed no respect to the Malays on the 12 May.* If you have been spat at in the face, and cursed, then you can understand the feelings of the Malays.

'The Malays whom you thought would not revolt have become maddened and run amok, sacrificing their lives, and they have killed people whom they hate because you have given these people too much face. The responsibility for the death of these people, both Muslims and Kafirs,† must inevitably be placed on leaders who hold warped opinions.

' . . . The fact is that now the Malays, regardless of whether they are in the PMIP or in UMNO, truly hate you, especially those who have been insulted by the Chinese and those who have lost their homes, children and relatives because of your compromising attitude.'

Thus a backbencher writes to his Prime Minister. When he accused the Tengku of compromise and blamed the moderate Alliance leaders for their 'warped opinions' he was holding them responsible for the May disturbances. With little logic, Mahathir went on to say that the Tengku's actions have increased 'the intensification of Malays' hatred towards the Government'.

It is not yet clear whether Mahathir was kicked out of the central executive simply because he challenged the Tengku's leadership or

* The day of the Opposition victory celebrations.
† Infidels.

68

because he had for so long championed the cause of the ultra-nationalists. Mahathir, until his expulsion, enjoyed wide publicity in the Malay-language press for his anti-Chinese and anti-Indian pronouncements. Not to have restrained him earlier appeared to indicate that the Tengku was losing his grip on both the UMNO party and the administration.

Any moves towards a multi-racial solution to Malaysia's difficulties naturally have not been welcomed by the 'ultras'. Tan Siew Sin's inclusion in the emergency cabinet was regarded by some observers as an indication that the Malays were still able to think in multi-racial terms but efforts to bring back Tan Siew Sin received no public support from anybody inside UMNO. Newspapers projecting UMNO views made a point of supporting Tan's original decision to withdraw. Mahathir was quoted as saying: 'If the MCA wants to make sure that they will be supported by the Chinese they will have to wait for another general election. . . . The MCA should accept the present situation that the majority of the Chinese do not support them.'

The comment of another UMNO leader was perhaps more significant. Relations between UMNO and the MIC (Malayan Indian Congress) would have to be reviewed, he said.

Mukhtaruddin Dazin, in his July 4 leaflet, maintained that the 'establishment of the National Operations Council was natural and should be preserved'. He continued: 'The Malays must not want a return to parliamentary rule. Malaya, through the NOC, must lead the country towards the aims of the national Malay philosophy. This can be carried out by expanding the armed forces loyal to the Malay race and by consolidating the unity of the Malays.

'When non-Malays fight for equal rights, Malays must . . . be offensive. They must fight to review the whole question of citizenship and *withdrawn** citizenship, by means of language tests, essay, religion and Malay customs (tests), based on the national Malay philosophy.

'Our present enemies are not only the Chinese and the Indians but also the Americans, British and Australians. In their discussions they have clearly sided with the Indians and the Chinese.

'We must find new friends who can adapt themselves to the methods of our new administration. Among these are Burma, Indonesia, Thailand, Kenya, revolutionary countries which have

* Original italics.

faced the fact that democracy is not workable in developing countries.

' .. With the will of God we have returned to a situation in which is possible to restore Malay sovereignty.'

This leaflet, Mahathir's letter to the Tengku, and four other similar documents were all banned by the Government under the Internal Security Act. Anyone 'publishing, printing, selling or distributing' any of the six papers is liable to three years' jail, a fine of M$2,000 or both. Possession can mean a year in prison and a fine.

Copies of some of them have been sent abroad and have been printed in various Asian newspapers. Mukhtaruddin's leaflet was reproduced in the Hong Kong *Sunday Post-Herald*.* Quite how much sympathy he thought would be evinced by Hong Kong's Chinese readers it is difficult to imagine. It could have been a gesture of childish defiance but these documents, no matter where they are circulated, do put forward the Malay extremists' views. By banning them, such views do not cease to exist and the opposition to the present UMNO leadership still continues.

The leaders of the UMNO extremists have seldom been named and they remain behind the scenes. The only two who are mentioned with any frequency are Sayed Jafhar Albar (who is thought to have agitated for the arrest of Lee Kuan Yew's cabinet in 1965, just before Singapore was forced out of Malaysia) and Sayed Nasir, for many years noted for his ultra-nationalist views. In August 1965, Mr Lee Kuan Yew posed a threat to the formation of a Malay-dominated Malaysia when his policy of seeking to build a modern nation (with the slogan 'Malaysia for Malaysians') received considerable applause and support. Singapore's withdrawal was inevitable but the Malaysian leaders in Kuala Lumpur did nothing to curb the influence of the 'ultras' within UMNO who continued to influence the fast-growing extremist faction. This influence cannot now be removed merely by sacking a backbencher of Mahathir's calibre.

The Tengku now has the support of the non-Malays, who regard him as the obvious Malay leader to attempt to restore some kind of multi-racial harmony. Whatever the value of non-Malay backing during these months following the riots it is quite clear that without continued Malay support the Tengku will not be able to hold the extremists in check. Tun Razak has either been unable to replace the

* Sunday, July 27, 1969.

Tengku or, for reasons of personal loyalty, does not wish to do so. He has performed aimlessly and, for many Malays, he has ceased to be the champion of the Malays' cause. Though he is still spoken of as Malaysia's 'strong man', his political stature has been diminished.

Tun Dr Ismail, who returned from retirement on the third day of the riots, is unlikely to contest Razak's position as the Tengku's Deputy. He is a leader of moderate views and his return gave some measure of comfort to the Chinese. But his recent statement that 'Western democracy is not the only kind of democracy; there are other kinds', has done little to strengthen his position in the eyes of non-Malays.

Rumour insists that, since he rejoined the Government, Ismail has been pressing for the arrest of Harun (Selangor's Chief Minister) and other sponsors of the original UMNO demonstration which began the disturbances. The same rumour maintains that Ismail is opposed by Tun Razak (who believes nothing is to be gained by accusing Harun) and this has resulted in a further dissension, this time within the ranks of the moderates themselves. While this is only rumour it is being spoken of too near the top to be disregarded.

If this latest dissension comes out into the open the multi-racial police will side with Dr Ismail and the Malay soldiery support Tun Razak. The friction between police and army was apparent all through the disturbances; it is likely that it will continue for as long as the NOC behaves as though it has something to conceal.

Towards the end of July, nine Malay student leaders, who claimed to represent 25,000 Malay students,* gave an interview to four foreign correspondents. Outlining their demands, they called for an all-Malay apartheid-style Government with the Chinese barred from taking part. The only condition on which they would allow Chinese to remain in Malaysia, they said, was under a one-race Government with all power and privileges in Malay hands. The Chinese community would lose their citizenship and the right to vote. If the Chinese resisted, the only alternative was all-out racial war.†

It is of some interest to note that these same student groups have, in the past, been swift to condemn any form of racial discrimination in South Africa and Rhodesia.

* The National Union of Muslim Students, the National Union of Malaysian Students and the Mara Institute of Technology Students Union. The combined membership of these three student bodies is over 27,000. The student leaders claimed near unanimous support of their members.
† Reuter report: Kuala Lumpur, July 20, 1969.

71

During this frank and sometimes alarming interview which lasted for nearly three hours the student leaders said Malays would fight to the death for a Malay-dominated nation. They boasted that students who had taken part in the disturbances were proud of their actions and that the death of Chinese schoolchildren was no more than the death of 'potential adults'.

Referring to Tengku Abdul Rahman (who is known as 'The Father of Malaysia') the students said: 'The Tengku is a great man who should have retired long ago in glory. Now he is regarded as a traitor by the Malays and is a hero only to the Chinese.'

They demanded that the Tengku step down 'before the end of the year' and insisted that their student demonstration on July 17 marked the beginning of a campaign to oust him. 'He must be ousted soon,' they said, and agreed that 'the end of the year would be too late', when asked how long they were prepared to wait.

A spokesman for the Government said these were extremist views which did not reflect those held by the great majority of students. This may be so; perhaps these student leaders did not have all the support they claimed but nevertheless they are in a position to control a sizeable section of Malay student opinion.

Nothing whatsoever is to be gained by denying the existence of extremist student opposition to the Tengku and to multi-racial policies. No Government leader has made any pronouncement about them at all. The four correspondents who interviewed the students subsequently tried to see Tun Razak and hear his comments on the students' demands. Tun Razak declined to see them.

In the middle of August the NOC announced the formation of a committee, which would study the University of Malaysia campus 'with a view to promoting community life among students'. This, apparently, was the result of a directive from Tun Razak to a newly formed department—The Department of National Unity—which had been told to 'make a thorough study of the aspirations of Malaysian youth and recommend measures to be taken'.*

By waiting for the reports of study committees much valuable time is being lost. By refusing to make statements, enforcing censorship and channelling all news through the bottleneck of the Information Co-ordination Centre, the authorities are encouraging rumour and untrue racist allegations. It is not surprising that banned letters and pamphlets circulate freely.

* *Straits Times*: August 15, 1969.

There is no doubt that the number of Malays who are dissatisfied with the Tengku's leadership has increased in recent months (as the election results in his own Kedah constituency clearly indicated) but, without the Tengku, Malaysia will have little chance of recovery. Non-Malay support is of small value to him; if he cannot continue to hold UMNO together, and retain the support of the Malays, his days as Prime Minister are limited.

BOYCOTT AND GOODWILL

One immediate effect of the disturbances has been an insidious boycott of Malay shops, foodstalls and markets by the Chinese. Malay coffee-shops have suffered; so, too, have small retailers, fruit farmers and stall owners. At the beginning of the odorous durian season, early in June, durian growers from outside Kuala Lumpur found it impossible to market their produce. Durian is a fruit much enjoyed by all races in the peninsula; it grows wild in kampong areas and is a good source of income for many kampong Malays. Even as far away as Singapore, people will not accept durian fruit from across the causeway.

Chinese decline to get into taxis driven by Malays; Chinese taxi-drivers will not stop for Malay fares. The famous Malay 'satay' stalls in Campbell Road are not patronised by the Chinese.

It is the Malays who suffer the most. Malays seldom eat in Chinese food-shops (because of the Muslims' aversion to pork); Malay shops and stalls, relying on Chinese and Indian patronage, have gone bankrupt. Chinese businessmen no longer wear the colourful, Malay-style batik shirts. No normal commerce between Chinese businessmen and Malay farmers has been restarted. The lines drawn through the whole pattern of society are battle lines.

In the short term, the economy has been buoyed up by the world demand for rubber and tin, Malaysia's main exports. In the last six months rubber prices have risen by over one-third—by 8d. a pound.

In the long term, unless a political solution is found quickly, the economy will suffer. The two main dangers are that foreign investment will be frightened away and that the Chinese economic boycott of Malay products will increasingly affect day-to-day business.

The emergency Cabinet has appealed for an end to the boycott. Selangor's Chief Minister Harun (the sponsor of the original UMNO demonstration) has asked the public not to boycott the shops of

73

'Malaysians of other races' but these appeals have had no effect. Racial bitterness remains.

If the National Operations Council, with its censorship, Emergency Regulations and 'do nothing' policy, allows this bitterness and hatred to remain permanently ingrained in Malaysian life then it is inevitable that foreign business concerns will become more hesitant about investing money in the country. The local Chinese can hardly be blamed if they are already reluctant to tie up their funds in new business projects when their future is insecure.

The Malay language newspaper, *Utusan Malaysia*, at the end of July,* criticised a report in the *Far Eastern Economic Review* which suggested that many Malaysian Chinese were trying to emigrate. In an editorial the paper said that the results of its own inquiries at the United States Embassy and the Canadian, Australian and New Zealand High Commissions did not support the contention that applications for immigration visas had greatly increased. The paper reminded all Malaysians that citizenship meant taking the good with the bad and was not just a matter of convenience.

*   *   *   *   *

Though present leaders apparently put great stress on the importance of goodwill meetings and Goodwill Committees these are not yet achieving any positive results. With the amount of tension apparent in Malaysia today there is no reason why, internally, these expressions of goodwill should have any effect whatsoever. They may have some marginal value in helping to improve Malaysia's image overseas.

A large photograph was displayed in the *Straits Times*, early in June, which showed a Chinese civilian presenting a scroll to the Commanding Officer, 5 Battalion, The Royal Malay Regiment. The caption to this picture said that the Chairman of the Chow Kit Road Goodwill Committee, grateful for the army's presence during the riots, presented the scroll which was inscribed: 'Thank you for looking after us during the disturbances.' The value of this sort of publicity could only be found abroad; within Malaysia it is laughed out of court.

There is an obvious need for the army to embark seriously on a Hearts and Minds programme in both urban and rural areas. However, there is no indication at all that this will even be

* *Utusan Malaysia*: Kuala Lumpur, July 30, 1969.

considered. During these months of political uncertainty, with racial tension stretched almost to breaking, neither the Malay soldiers nor the Chinese and Indian civilians would be likely to take much notice of any gestures of goodwill made half-heartedly.

SINGAPORE, MALAYSIA AND EXTERNAL DEFENCE
Singapore is watching Malaysia with some anxiety; the events of recent months will continue to give Mr Lee Kuan Yew justifiable concern. Once again the Malays are testing his statesmanship. Singapore restraint has so far been admirable.

Singapore obviously fears a renewed outbreak of communist insurgency in Malaya which would at once affect the economy of the island republic. Naturally, too, Singapore must be concerned at the prospect of an all-Malay Government to the north as well as the Indonesians to the south. Singapore would indeed become the walnut in the crackers.

When the race riots began in Malaysia the tensions and anxiety were at once evident in Singapore. The Singapore Government's concern lest the conflict spilled across the causeway that links the two countries, is readily understood. Chinese youths from Malaysia threatened retaliation attacks against Singapore Malays (who are in a small minority). When some outbreaks of racial violence did occur, the manner in which the authorities dealt with them showed that Singapore had learned lessons which Kuala Lumpur had not thought necessary to study. Multi-racial security forces, on stand-by alert, quickly clamped down on the rioters with complete impartiality. Although four people were killed the island was back to normal within days; confidence was restored and no permanent damage was done to racial harmony.

Singapore's external defence is closely tied to Malaysia's. This will become more complicated after the planned British withdrawal from south-east Asia in 1971. Singapore is unlikely to remain inactive if the Malaysian Government is overtaken by the influences of communist subversion which are now at work in the peninsula.

The Tengku has said: 'We are naturally nervous at being left alone after the British withdrawal and if there is any friendly gesture by Australia or New Zealand we will jump at it.'* But the Five Power† defence talks held in Canberra last June were dis-

* Reuter report: Kuala Lumpur, 12 August, 1969.
† Malaysia, Singapore, Australia, New Zealand and Britain.

75

appointing for the Malays who wanted firmer promises. A Malaysian spokesman said after the conference that there had been 'doubts and difficulties' over the future defence of Malaysia and the doubts had not been resolved. 'Even some basic issues' still caused disagreement.

Malaysia's dispute with the Philippines over the ownership of Sabah territory added to the difficulties since Australia is allied to the Philippines under the South-East Asia Treaty Agreement. The Australian Prime Minister's pointed reference to the defence of 'Malaya' and not 'Malaysia' gave rise to some bitter comment in Kuala Lumpur.

The first communist insurrection took more than a decade to put down and the Malaysian Government is clearly in no position to cope with a second Emergency. The British would not come to their aid again and the Americans, after their experience in Vietnam, are unlikely to become involved. The Australians and the New Zealanders could only hope to contain a communist-terrorist campaign in its earliest stages. Their reluctance to commit themselves to the defence of Malaysia or Singapore is understandable. So, too, must be their concern over the Malaysians' inability to resolve their difficulties and put their house in order.

Addressing members of the 3 Battalion, Royal Malay Regiment, at the beginning of August, the Tengku said that Malaysia was now expanding her armed forces 'in view of the British withdrawal and the uselessness of the five-power defence arrangements'. He added that, at the Canberra talks, Australia and New Zealand had shown themselves to be 'not too keen to take the responsibility of the defence of this region'. Malaysia had therefore to find some alternative security arrangements and adopt a more realistic and friendly policy towards her neighbour.*

Malaysia was now getting good support from Indonesia and Thailand and hoped to get good support from Singapore, the Tengku said, stressing that the communists were the country's main enemy, both on the Thai border and along the Sarawak border with Indonesia.

Many Malay politicians in Kuala Lumpur are now beginning to feel that the country cannot go on, indefinitely, policing and financing the Borneo States and that, before long, it might be necessary to consider dissolving Malaysia and leaving Sabah and Sarawak to fend for themselves.

* AP and Reuter: Kuala Lumpur, August 1, 1969.

The May riots resulted in the postponement of the elections in the Borneo States. The decision to postpone them was strongly criticised, especially in Sarawak where resentment against Kuala Lumpur's domination has always been in evidence. The suspension of the elections did not result in open defiance but Sarawak and Sabah are waiting to see what happens in West Malaysia. The commonly expressed fear that 'the elections will never be held' continues to underscore the distrust and suspicion Sarawakians have for the peninsular Malays.

If Malaysia falls apart Sarawak can hardly hope to become an independent, viable nation and would need to form a federation with Sabah and the wealthy, independent State of Brunei. Despite the concern of Chinese in Sarawak there would be little reason for them to fear an immediate Indonesian takeover if Malaysia broke up. Indonesia is not likely to want to absorb into her own territory an unsympathetic, undeveloped, rural community. Yet the threat of a takeover by Indonesia will remain since Sarawak, more than any other part of south-east Asia, is wide open to communist subversion and could quickly be receptive to Peking's directives.

By 1971 the British military presence in south-east Asia will have been withdrawn; the vast American commitment in Vietnam will probably have been phased out. By then Malaysia could be in the grip of a second communist insurrection. On the stability of Malaysia rests the stability of the whole south-east Asian region. The May disturbances and the Malay leaders' inability to bring the country back to peace and normality give little cause for south-east Asian's future to be awaited with confidence.

*   *   *   *   *

Malay leaders are concerned with the hypothetical threat of external danger, yet the very real threat is from the danger within and this should be consuming all their energy.

If the May riots had been merely a spontaneous clash between rival groups of Chinese and Malays this would have been serious enough; regrettably it was far more serious and the situation, as a result, is critical.

The Chinese believe that there were those in authority who connived at a planned attack and encouraged the Malays' savagery. They cannot be blamed for believing this. They have seen Malay troops enforcing the curfew with bias and discrimination; they have heard Government ministers brand all Opposition supporters as 'communists', 'anti-national' and 'disloyal'. They have watched Chinese be arrested, in their thousands, while the Malay attackers have remained unpunished. They know that it was a Malay UMNO demonstration that started the killings on May 13.

At the end of June, in Kuala Lumpur, I asked a number of young Chinese boys what lessons they had learned from the May disturbances.

They gave me five answers:

We can never again trust the Malays—not even the urban Malays whom we know.

We must band ourselves together and live in the same areas.

The soldiers cannot be trusted and we must arm ourselves against them.

Though the police behaved better than the soldiers still the police are suspect and we cannot trust even the non-Malay in the police force.

No matter what happens to us now and no matter what action the Government takes to improve things, there will never be any future in Malaysia for us or our children. (The average age of these youths was 23.)

In direct contrast, a group of young Malays said: 'Lessons learned? *We've* taught the *Chinese* a lesson. And the Indians too. If they need to be taught another lesson we'll do it again!'

On a foundation of suspicion and ill-will such as this, the Tengku and the moderate leaders have got to build again. Somehow the Chinese must be brought back into the Government. Leaders whom the Chinese community respect must take their share in running the country—and be seen to shoulder their responsibilities. Until the Chinese have their faith and confidence in Malaysia restored the country will continue on the brink of further violence and disorder, the threat of communist insurgency will increase each day and the stability of south-east Asia will remain in the balance.

Mr John Gorton, Australia's Prime Minister, said on June 4 that the sooner 'the even hand of justice' was extended to all Malaysians the better it would be. There is yet no sign at all that Malay leaders are unanimously of the same opinion.

The Malays and the Chinese have quarrelled for several decades.

Their ways of life are radically different and these differences are bound to persist; but there is no reason why the two communities should not both prosper, side by side.

While bringing the Chinese back into the administration, the policy of the Malaysian Government must be to put the strongest possible emphasis on economic development (as Mr Lee Kuan Yew has done successfully in Singapore). Tun Razak has outlined a more positive approach to the problem of foreign investment and given details of new agriculture and rural development policies. But this does not begin to get to the root of the difficulties.

The tasks confronting the Tengku and Tun Razak are great; they may indeed be too great for them to accomplish. Offers of co-operation from the Opposition parties have been rejected and the Chinese have little say in the emergency Cabinet or the National Operations Council. The Malays are being placated and, so far, there is nothing to indicate that the Chinese will be brought back to play a meaningful role in the administration. Racial tension and hatred are worse now than at any time in the country's history.

Rule by Royal Proclamation is not a solution. Nothing will be achieved by the Malaysian Government's present negative policies but if anybody is able to create order out of this chaotic situation it will be Tengku Abdul Rahman. No other leader has emerged who has either sufficient experience or who is capable of commanding the respect of all three racial groups.

Foreign correspondents reported the biased behaviour of Malay troops during the riots and the Government dismissed these reports as 'irresponsible'. Yet it was this bias which underscored the most explosive aspect of the whole disturbances. The tendency for one half of the population to regard the security forces as 'the enemy' has been the result of that bias. If racial conflict becomes a permanent feature of everyday life Malaysia will be torn apart by racial war. The bogy of communist insurrection, used to explain away the rioting, will then become a tragic reality.

Postscript:

While this book is still in preparation Tengku Abdul Rahman has published his account of the disturbances. It is called *May 13– Before & After*; in it the Tengku lays the blame for the riots squarely on the communists and the Opposition parties. He asserts that

79

communist funds, from Singapore, helped finance the opposition campaigns; the 'millions of dollars' used by the PMIP, he writes, 'certainly came from somewhere'. He accuses foreign correspondents of giving a 'disgusting display of irresponsible reporting' and of filing stories 'without even attempting to verify the truth'. He maintains that one quarter of Malaysia's four million Chinese 'owe allegiance, in whole or in part, to Mao Tse-tung's China'.

'The problem in this country,' the Tengku writes, 'is not really a Chinese problem, as others are wont to say, because the Chinese as a whole care mainly for their success in business and their well-being in an atmosphere of law and order.' It would seem, from this conclusion, that no lessons have been learned and that the real causes of the May riots in Kuala Lumpur have not been considered. The major problems are still being ignored.

After reading the Tengku's account I find there is nothing I have written in this book which I wish to amend or to qualify.

APPENDIX A

Arrivals of Chinese in Singapore:

1870	14,000
1875	31,000
1880	50,000
1890	95,000
1895	190,000
1900	200,000
1912	250,000

'The number of new arrivals varied thereafter between 150,000 and 250,000 a year, until in 1927 a record arrival of 360,000 Chinese was registered. In the thirty-two years between 1895 and 1927, six million Chinese had come in.

'These figures (given in round numbers) are taken from the Annual Reports of the Straits Settlements. It should be noted that they are *not* numbers of migrants to Malaya but merely to Singapore. Many migrated elsewhere, to Java in particular.'

A History of Modern Malaya: T. G. Tregonning (p. 174).

APPENDIX B

NATIONAL OPERATIONS COUNCIL

Director of Operations — Tun Razak

Council Members:

Tun Dr Ismail — Minister of Home Affairs

Tun Tan Siew Sin — President of the MCA

Tun Sambanthan — Minister of Works, Post & Telecoms (& President of MIC)

Enche Hamzah bin— Minister of Information & Broadcasting
Dato Abu Samah

Tunku Osman Jiwa— Chief of Armed Forces Staff

Tan Sri Salleh — Inspector-General of Police

Tan Sri Ghazali — Permanent Secretary, Ministry of
bin Shafie — Foreign Affairs

Chief Executive Officer — Lt. Gen. Dato Ibrahim bin Ismail, Director of Operations, West Malaysia

Assistants: — Enche Abdul Rahman Hamidon,
Deputy Secretary, Ministry of Defence
Lt. Col. Ghazali bin Che Mat,
Ministry of Defence
Superintendent Shariff bin Omar,
Royal Malaysia Police
Enche Yusoff bin Abdul Rashid,
Attorney-General's Office